WE

CANNOT
BUT TELL

WE CANNOT BUT TELL

A PRACTICAL GUIDE TO HEART TO HEART EVANGELISM

ROSS TOOLEY

Frontline Communications ● A Division of
Youth With A Mission
P.O. Box 55787
Seattle, Washington 98155

WE CANNOT BUT TELL

Published by Frontline Communications, a division of Youth With A Mission; P.O. Box 55787; Seattle, Washington 98155.

Scripture taken from the HOLY BIBLE, NEW INTERNATIONAL VERSION. Copyright © 1973, 1978, 1984 International Bible Society. Used by permission of Zondervan Bible Publishers.

ISBN 0-9615-5343-X

Printed in the United States of America.

10 9 8 7 6 5 4 3 2 1
95 94 93 92 91 90 89 88

To the people of the Philippines
whose grace, affection and hospitality
have affected my life forever.

CONTENTS

FOREWORD

When I first met Ross Tooley in 1967, I was impressed with his commitment to the Lord and his faith to launch new things for God. In his 21 years with Youth With A Mission (YWAM) I have had ample opportunity to observe him as I have worked alongside him in various capacities—even on one occásion in hut to hut evangelism among Hindus in the country of Fiji.

Ross is a missionary pioneer who has had extensive experience in frontline, eye to eye evangelism. It was Ross who, at the end of a fireworks display in Tonga, for example, started a street meeting among the crowds who had gathered for the coronation celebrations for their king. Due to the interest aroused, he then preached from the base of a flagpole and encouraged others to do the same. The gospel was shared with hundreds that night, altar calls were given and people who responded were prayed for. This scene and others similar have been repeated many, many times as Ross has ministered around the world.

I met a man at Billy Graham's conference for itinerant evangelists in 1986, who is a leader of a missionary organization in the Philippines. He shared with me how he was won to Christ by Ross Tooley in the Philippines some 15 years prior, and owes the ministry he has today to Ross's input into his life. (Ross led the work of YWAM in the

Philippines for ten years.)

As a teacher of the Word of God, Ross shares from his heart out of a great wealth of experience and relationship with God. When it comes to evangelism, he knows what he is talking about. I highly recommend Ross and this book for your growth and edification.

Loren Cunningham
President
Youth With A Mission

"They called them in again and commanded them not to speak or teach in the name of Jesus. But Peter and John replied . . . We cannot but tell of what we've seen and heard" (Paraphrase of Acts 4:18-20).

BEFORE WE BEGIN ...

The rush of air through the windows of the jeep was a welcomed blessing as we drove along the road near the heart of Manila, in the Philippines. We had been inching our way in congested traffic and the combination of this and the hot tropical sun had been an appalling mix. But the street we were driving along was now wide and although traffic was heavy by standards elsewhere in the world, we were able to move at a nice cooling speed. As we traveled beside the brown waters of the Pasig River to our left, I began to wonder why all the traffic appeared to be coming from the opposite direction. I hadn't remembered seeing any one-way signs.

To the right stood the huge market where Filipinos buy everything from vegetables to lobsters and from cheap hardware and trinkets to basketware and white rice. I loved it here in the Philippines! Along the side of this very wide street, bare-backed men wearing rubber slippers pushed carts full of cabbage, cans of water or blocks of ice. Although I came to Manila frequently, it was not often that my wife, Margaret and I were in Manila together, for our home at that time was five hours away in a mountain city 5000 feet above sea-level....

Then suddenly I saw him—a traffic officer signaling us

to stop. I pulled over to the side of the road.

"Good afternoon," I offered.

"Excuse me, sir," he politely replied, "Where are you going?"

"Just a couple of more blocks," I said with a wave of my arm.

He paused for just a moment, then said, "Then drive carefully. This is a one-way street, and you might get hit!"

As this incident indicates, a non-confrontational, accommodating, friendship-orientation exists more strongly in the non-Western world than it does in the West. And that's not all. There are many other values that predominate and pervade every aspect of these societies. Even a little knowledge of their values is very useful before embarking on the exciting adventure of preaching Christ in this segment of the world. I wish I had known these things, when, as a 19-year-old, I boarded the S.S. Oronsay to sail for the Philippines for the first time on February 14, 1966. Let's look then, at some of the major differences in the ways Westerners and non-Westerners think.[1]

1) Non-Westerners are more relative-oriented than absolute-oriented.

Just consider the incident about the traffic officer in Manila. Had the Filipino officer sent me back the other way, it would have taken about twenty minutes of "fighting-the-traffic" through clogged streets to have reached our destination. With the blessing of the policeman however, it only took us minutes to get where we wanted to go. Since the road was very wide at that point, and since man-pushed carts go up that street the wrong way, it wasn't that difficult (or dangerous!) for me to dodge the on-coming traffic. The officer was trying to be helpful. He probably didn't want to embarrass me by saying I was doing something wrong.

Obviously the extent to which non-Westerners are relative-oriented, varies depending on how far the prevailing religion of the culture deviates from the Word of God.

The philosophy of Hinduism, for example, is considered the furthest removed from the beliefs of Christianity. It is in Hindu areas, therefore, that the contrast between absolutes and relatives is so clearly marked. A man steeped in Hindu philosophy will consider truth to be saying "what the other person wants to hear," rather than the actual facts themselves. Hinduism teaches that lying is perfectly in order when protecting life or property or even so that lust can be expressed.

2) Non-Westerners are event-oriented, not time-oriented.

Most cultures have their tolerance threshold for tardiness, although in many Western circles there is no tolerance at all. In other Western areas it is a mere five or ten minutes. This tolerance factor is much greater in certain parts of Asia, Africa, the Pacific Islands and Latin America. It is usually culturally permissible in the Philippines, for example, to be 20 to 30 minutes late. But I have been in a part of Indonesia where church members arrived for a service one hour late every time. Then, in some parts of the non-Western world where time is measured in months instead of minutes, it is very acceptable to arrive two days or even two weeks late! Many times this is because transport and communications are scarce or even non-existent. Partly due to the fact of their having been raised from birth this way, and partly because of their orientation to people more than goals, certain non-Westerners tend to think, "As long as we have the event, so what if it doesn't start on time!"

3) Non-Westerners are more fellowship-oriented than goal-oriented.

We in the West can learn so much from our non-Western brothers. It is true that we have comfortable standards of living and we have advanced in technology to conquer outer space. But we haven't conquered where it really counts. When it comes to *inner space,* a non-Westerner usually wins hands down. Dr. Billy Graham has said that loneliness is the greatest problem in our society. Dr. James Hodge, a professor at Northeastern Ohio University says this about the problem: "The major underlying reason is that people are so achievement-oriented, so wrapped up in themselves, so focused on their personal interests that they're unable to make or maintain healthy, close relationships."[2]

What we're seeing today is the results of the "me" generation. The problem has been aggravated by the obsession to succeed, to have material possessions and be a winner, and we have been successful in this area. We have our material possessions all right, but they have come with a fearsome price tag. In the drive for success we have alienated people, including even our loved ones. As a result, we are lonely. America has the highest rate for teenage suicides in the world with 1000 attempts a day.[3] We also have the highest divorce rate in the Western world for Christians.

True, it is godly to have goals. But it becomes ungodly if those goals isolate us from people and from the flow of emotional energy that comes from being properly related to others—many others in fact. Here many a non-Westerner is a shining example to us. He loves other people's company and there is always room for one more. In having a number of non-Westerners on teams I have lead over the years, I have found it is necessary to allow time for ample fellowship, fun and laughter. In leading the YWAM base in Baguio City in the Philippines for many years for example, I found I needed to declare a holiday every now and then, even for half a day so we could sit around, drink coffee and have fellowship. They all loved that. More than that, they needed those times of interaction in a relaxed atmosphere.

4) The non-Westerner is not a confronter.

From childhood he is taught not to confront. He is taught to conform and is discouraged from being different from others. He is particularly discouraged from confronting a person older than himself, for in most non-Western cultures, if you are older, you are inevitably considered right. Therefore, if you are younger you are always wrong. This means that if there is a disagreement, the younger must apologize to the older even if the younger is in the *right!* Obviously we are talking about the culture at large and not Christianity within that culture. But even so, it is amazing how much of this thinking infiltrates the church in these societies.

While we in the West find it easier to confront, we need to remember two things. Firstly, not all of us obey Mt. 18:15 anyway. That Scripture reads, "If your brother sins against you, go and show him his fault, just between the two of you." That command must be one of the most disobeyed of all. Secondly, when we do confront we often do it in the wrong spirit which can even be worse than not confronting at all. "Truth not obeyed in the Spirit of truth, is not truth," says Loren Cunningham, the Founder and President of Youth With A Mission.

To confront then, is a biblical command and an important ingredient to a mentally healthy life. But we also have to remember that, if we do it vindictively, we will wound and maim people emotionally. We must not forget the admonition of the apostle Paul who wrote, "Brothers, if someone is caught in a sin, you . . . should restore him *gently.* But watch yourself, or you also may be tempted." When a non-Westerner learns to confront, it is usually a beautiful thing, because he does it so gently. We Westerners have so much to learn here.

5) A non-Westerner is group-oriented, not individualistic.

Over the centuries, the non-Westerner has learned that for emotional and financial considerations, as well as for reasons of physical protection, it is better to be group-oriented. This contrasts sharply with the rugged individualism and obsession with personal rights and freedoms of people in the West—particularly those from the United States. The Westerner needs to see that group-orientation is so ingrained into a non-Westerner that it is impossible for him not to think of others and that is *healthy*. We have already caught a glimpse of what a mess the "me" generation has made of society with the emphasis on individuality. However, the non-Westerner must recognize that one day he will stand before the judgment throne of Christ as an *individual*. Where group-orientation is unhealthy is when we bow to things that are against the will of God out of deference to others.

Because of his orientation, the non-Westerner usually works best in the context of a group. Therefore, when he comes to the Lord and his original clan rejects him, or when his family are out to kill him because he is leaving his traditional religion, he must join a new group. But a non-Westerner must also belong to a group even when there are not the extreme circumstances just described. Emotionally he is not always equipped to handle living the Christian life alone. We make a mistake in evangelism in the non-Western world, I believe, when we win someone to the Lord, have him enjoy our fellowship and the emotional satisfaction of our acceptance, and then *leave* him by himself when our evangelism tour is over. It is my view that he needs to be introduced as quickly as possible after his conversion to a church or long-term group. This is so there will not be the traumatic experience of being emotionally torn when the short-termers leave. When teams haven't left non-Westerners bonded into a long-term group, the best possible result hasn't been achieved. Sometimes negative effects have been the result.

6) A Non-Westerner expects his parents (or leader) to anticipate his needs.

Although the non-Westerner is required by his culture to accept the fact that his elders are always right, there is a definite trade-off, for he receives something in return. His elders assume certain responsibilities for him—one of them being that they will try to anticipate his needs without being told. This, therefore, makes deference to those who are older or who are in authority much easier. Unfortunately, we as Westerners don't always realize this. Neither do we always understand that because we are foreigners, we are regarded as elders or at least older brothers in some cultures. If you are a leader over a non-Westerner you must accept his having certain expectations. One of them will be that you will be sensitive to his needs. And remember, he is not confrontational. He won't necessarily come and tell you all about those needs. He may feel very disappointed when you do not notice them even if you cannot meet them. Be patient with him and realize that for some strange reason, it always helps us if someone notices our needs even if that person is unable to satisfy them, no matter in *what* culture we find ourselves.

Naturally there are variations of all that we have discussed. The extent to which all the foregoing varies, depends on the amount of influences a particular people group has received from the religious and philosophical teachings around it or from the colonial power that formerly governed it. But, by and large, you will find the six characteristics mentioned above mark all non-Western countries around the world.[1]

Whenever we enter a new culture we must refrain from saying, "This is crazy." Instead we are to look beyond what we're observing and search for the reason for what we see. It may not be logical to the Western mind. It may not line up scripturally, but usually we can come to an understanding of *why* things are done the way they are. After all, we are seeing just the tip of the iceberg. The reasons can be buried very deep below. With understanding comes compassion. And when compassion is present, the non-Westerner is released more readily to make an effort to obey the biblical principles we are trying to expound. When they see our love and not our criticism, they will even overlook the most horrendous offensive cultural mistakes that we make, and we Westerners all make them. Obviously it takes time to learn all these things, but learn them we must. But while we are learning them, we must be patient. As we recognize the strengths of the non-Western culture, we should also be gently pointing out the strengths of the biblical patterns (but not necessarily the things we like about American or European cultures). Obviously the non-Westerner must be sensitively instructed to look more to God for his needs, and not just to his leader. This doesn't come overnight. Remember, if the non-Westerner recognizes that you love and enjoy him, he will be your friend for the rest of your life.[4]

---

1. The use of the term non-Westerner here and elsewhere in this book means those peoples usually living in Asia, Africa, the Pacific Islands or Latin America. The term Third-Worlder is not used very much in this book because a number of non-Western nations are First-World countries financially.

2. The National Enquirer, March 26, 1985, p. 53.

3 Lloyd Billingsley, "Half in Love with Easeful Death," Eternity Magazine, March 1985 issue, p. 28.

4. If you wish to know more about the ways of the non-Westerner there are a number of books around on this subject. A classic on the subject is "Communicating Christ Cross-Culturally," by Dave Hesselgrave. You could also look for the forthcoming book, "Asia: A Christian Perspective," by Mary Ann Lind of Pacific & Asia Christian University (PACU), and a forthcoming book on cross-cultural relations, by David Hall, also of PACU.

I. PREPARING OUR HEARTS

Chapter One

WHY PERSONAL EVANGELISM?

I suddenly looked at my watch.

Oh, no.

It was the day before a holiday period in the nation of Sri Lanka and I needed to get Traveler's Checks cashed. In ten minutes the banks were going to close for three days.

I jumped on the next big red double-decker bus to get to the bank just as fast as I could. It was my responsibility to cash these checks for the Youth With A Mission team of which I was a part. It could prove awkward for the entire team to have insufficient Sri Lankan Rupees for three days. I looked at my watch. *I should still just make it to the bank in time,* I thought. Finally the huge bus shuddered to a halt near the branch of the Bank of Ceylon and I quickly jumped out. *Oh, no!* The iron gate at the bank's entrance had been drawn closed. A young Sri Lankan dressed entirely in white controlled the gate. When I asked to be let in he refused. Now desperate and feeling responsible to those I was traveling with, I asked to see the manager. The young man's eyes opened in amazement.

"Do you know the manager?" he asked incredulously. I didn't, but I couldn't afford to let him know that.

"I want to see the manager," is all I said. He slid the iron concertina gate to one side and let me in. I was then ushered into the head office where I explained what I needed. Soon an officer was attending my need while I continued to sit at the wooden desk opposite the manager in a small office. Perhaps obliged to make small talk, he spoke.

"What are you doing in Sri Lanka?" he asked. I told him that a group of us were in the country telling people about the Lord Jesus Christ.

"Who is paying your way?" A banker would have to be interested in that question! I shared how we were all responsible for our own expenses. Some of us looked to God for that supply. Sensing the timing was right I then politely asked him a question, hoping that this might lead into a witnessing situation.

"Are you interested in spiritual matters?" I offered. The obviously well-educated man with a slightly sad expression didn't appear that interested.

We nonetheless talked back and forth for a while. I found myself searching for a way to make clear to him that by itself his nominal church background was not enough. Meanwhile bank officers dressed in white were walking back and forth through this office as we talked. Finally I asked, "Would you then say that you are a friend of God's?"

I was quite unprepared for his response. Raising both his arms above his head right there in his office, this otherwise unexcitable banker exclaimed, "I would give anything in the world to be God's friend and have peace of mind!"

That was the entrance to his heart. The feeling of being cheated financially by others, he was to tell me, was plaguing him, filling him with bitterness. The need he *felt* was freedom from resentment and the depression that went with it. His real need, of course, was to get to know God as his Father. Yet despite his plight, there was no indication that he wanted to give his life over to the Lord.

Finally one of the dressed-all-in-white bank officers walked into the office and then correctly and politely handed me the Sri Lankan Rupees in exchange for the Traveler's Checks. I could be so grateful for the fact that cashing money in a developing nation takes time. The fifteen minutes I had sat there had given me an opportunity to witness to this man in a meaningful way. Now, because of how the conversation had gone, I was loathe to just leave it at that. He had opened his heart to me and I felt he was somewhat ready for the gospel so I asked if I could see him again. The result was an invitation for my wife and I to have dinner with him in his home after the coming holiday had ended. I left delighted at how this trip to the bank had gone. My meeting with Melville the banker had indeed been a *divine appointment.*

The following week Margaret and I sat down to a meal with Melville and his wife. Wanting to be very hospitable, they had gone out of their way to place crab in front of us which was so spicy hot that Margaret and I had to eat lots of rice and bananas to keep our mouths even somewhat cool! We did appreciate their sincere hospitality. Melville and Mavis lived in a nice house by Sri Lankan standards but it was not lavish. After the meal, we retired to an area near the dining room table where tea was served. Because they were from a nominal Christian background we were able to share the Scriptures with them both, and at the end of the evening he bought one of the New Testaments we were selling as a team. We invited them to come to some special meetings that we were going to hold at a church in town.

He came one evening when it was my turn to speak. That night I spoke on the awfulness of sin and the cruel death of Christ on the cross so man may be reconciled to the Father. When I made the altar call, he came right to the front, and knelt for prayer. It wasn't because my sermon was so marvelous. Much later he was to share with me that our *time together in his home* had been the thing that had attracted him to the Lord.

We have kept in touch with Melville over the last 16 years and have stayed with him in his home as we've passed through that country. On one occasion he traveled to the Philippines to spend two months sharing his testimony and going out with one of our evangelistic teams to the highlands of Northern Luzon. On bank business abroad he has often visited nearby Youth With A Mission (YWAM) bases and in 1985 went through a Discipleship Training School, run by YWAM in Canada. He is certainly a different man from the one I first met.

In fact, he was to tell me later that he'd had thoughts of suicide at the time I'd first met him. And he even wonders if he might have eventually taken the advice of his friends and hired a killer to get even with those who had cheated him.

Witnessing for Christ then, is a fulfilling experience which has its own special rewards. Whether its the bank manager from Sri Lanka or other *divine appointments*— like the New Zealand housewife who was about to burn her house down before we led her to Christ, or the university student who is now a pastor or the young lady who came to faith on board an airline flight—everyone you lead to the Lord holds a special place in your heart.

But doing things for God just to be fulfilled or even to help people cannot be our overriding reason for evangelism. It has to be rooted more deeply than that. Let's look then at some of the other compelling reasons why we should be a witness for the Lord Jesus Christ.

1) It is the will of God.

I am reminded here of the British doctor who was once riding a train while holidaying in the Middle East. Suddenly the train shuddered violently as the engineer desperately tried to bring the train to a standstill. This was followed by the doctor's horror-filled realization that several of the other carriages were leaving the tracks. He could not only see the mechanical wreckage, but he could hear the human sounds of groaning and shouting as well.

Shaken but unhurt, the doctor managed to get out of his compartment and began walking alongside the ill-fated train with its twisted cars. Bleeding people were emerging from the mechanical chaos amid the sounds of others who were groaning in pain. As more and more people were helped out of their badly wrecked cars, the doctor quickly assessed the situation. Beside the tracks lay human beings—hurting, bleeding and dying. Finally it became too much for him.

"If only I had my instruments! If only I had my instruments," he cried out in anguish. "If only I had my instruments, I could save these people!"

God must say the same thing at times. As He looks down upon a world of human chaos brought about by man's inhumanity to man, He must feel deep within His loving heart an even more profound anguish than that of the doctor. His instruments, of course, are dedicated Christians, who in loving obedience move into the sea of human need surrounding them. It is a God of justice who gives us the biblical injunction, "Go into all the world and preach the good news to all creation" (Mark 16:15).

2) We must go where the people are.

Evangelism as Jesus intended, was to meet people and win them on their own ground—at their businesses, in their homes, at the office, by the beach or while traveling by public transportation. In other words, we should be reaching both friends and strangers for Christ during routine and recreational life. I have found that in many ways this kind of witnessing has been more effective because it's done in a more natural setting and people have been less on the defensive. (In a later chapter we will discuss moving a conversation in these situations from the natural to the spiritual.) This is not to say that we should do away with organized witnessing drives into the parks, streets, jails, or hospitals. If we are led by God's Spirit we can, with experience, be just as natural in these situations as well.

Not that this does away with preaching, for *both* public proclamation and personal witnessing are mentioned in the New Testament. It is from the extreme of just leaving evangelism to full-time Christian workers however, that the Body of Christ must turn. Everybody needs to be involved if we are going to get the job done.

It is my view that most of evangelism was originally intended by the Lord to be done during the week outside
church meetings, because this is where the sinners are to
be found. Our Sundays, I believe, were supposed to be
more a day for the edification and education of Christians
and a time when we introduce to our fellowships those we
have brought to the Lord during the week. My point here
is that we are to be witnessing for Christ in the workaday
world. We must not leave it to the initiative of the unsaved
to come to our special meetings. Let's take the message to
them!

3) We must show interest and concern for people.

Many today carry in their hearts deep-seated frustrations,
fears and wounds. It may be some horrifying experience or
an injustice that has been dealt them. It may also be
loneliness or plain boredom. Whatever it may be, their
response to us and the gospel we present will often depend
on whether we genuinely care. Jesus demonstrated He
cared as the following story reveals.

He was on the road with his disciples one day, traveling from Judea on a three-day journey to the province of
Galilee (John 4:3-42). He had decided to take the route
through a region inhabited by a race of people called
Samaritans who were of mixed blood. The antagonism between these two races was such that the Samaritans often
refused overnight shelter to Jews who were passing
through their territory. When the Samaritans denied Jesus
and his party lodging for the night on one occasion, James
and John asked Jesus for permission to call down fire upon
them (Luke 9:54). Anger towards the Samaritans thus
seethed even in the breasts of Jesus' disciples—an
animosity that reflected their cultural bias. The Jews felt
the Samaritans "unclean," and would certainly not use any
dish that a Samaritan had used.

When the party reached the town of Sychar around

noon one day, Jesus, tired from His journey, sat by the well while the disciples went to get food. As Jesus sat resting, one of these Samaritans, a woman, approached the well to draw water. How then, should Jesus as a Jew react in the presence of one of these despised people? This is interesting. The answer is simple. In order to show interest and concern, He obviously had to break the uncaring conventions of his race which were as follows: In the first place no Jew had unnecessary dealings with a Samaritan. Secondly, Jesus would have to ignore the Jewish tradition of being ceremonially unclean by drinking from a Samaritan vessel if he were to request a drink to quench his middle-of-the-day-thirst. Thirdly, Jewish religious teachers rarely spoke with women in public. Women and children were despised. Lastly, He would be doing a "no-no" to have anything to do with this woman who (as the story unfolds) was living in an adulterous relationship. But for Jesus, it was more important to demonstrate His love than to conform to the ungodly aspects of the Jewish culture of the day.

"I'd like a drink," He said politely. "Do you think you could let me drink out of your dipping container?"

The woman was astounded.

"But you're a Jew, and I am a Samaritan woman. How can you ask me for a drink?"

This is how He had opened the conversation. He did not scold her, but spoke to her in a kind way which increased her sense of self-worth. Then gently and uncompromisingly he led her to the reality of her sins. Here was a woman who had failed in five marriage relationships and who must have been minus 500 on the self-esteem scale. But, by showing interest and concern, Jesus wooed this woman to faith without compromising the commandment concerning adultery which he upheld. Then something else happened as this woman became excited about the Christ. Instead of denying Jesus and His party hospitality, other Samaritans were actually urging Him to stay with them in the village! What an unprecedented outreach on Samaritan soil! How excited Jesus must have been to have overcome the Samaritan's prejudice and to have illustrated

to the disciples how to operate caringly in evangelism.
Many more came to the Lord as a result of His two days in
that village (John 4:39-42). And it all started when Jesus
showed interest in one lowly person. The world will be won
faster if we would all follow the example Jesus set for us
here.

The greatest argument for the need to personally convey the gospel is the overall example that God Himself
gave. When He desired to communicate the message of
salvation He set us a pattern. He did not set up a
loudspeaker network over the world and address the
human race by it. What then, did He do? "The Word became *flesh* and made his dwelling among us. We have seen
his glory . . . " (John 1:14).

In turn, when Jesus had accomplished His mission and
was about to return to heaven after his triumphant resurrection, He announced His will for the disciples: "As the
Father has sent me, I am sending you" (John 20:21). In exactly the same way that the message of God became flesh
and blood in Jesus, we have been commissioned by Christ
to take that message in flesh and blood. That means taking
God's news to the people under the scorching sun, down
dusty pathways and to those whom society considers outcasts. It means sitting cross-legged on dirty floors and
befriending drop-outs. It means sharing Christ personally
with rich and poor, old and young, male and female,
everywhere, at any time. Just as people saw the glory of
God in Christ, so must they *see* the reality of God in us.

Outsiders are going to more readily see God by way of
our genuine love and concern, our gracious speech, and
our gentle words. In our YWAM crusades, it is not always
the Bible College graduate with the correct *words* who
wins more people to Christ. It is the person with the most
caring *lifestyle*. It is the one with the ability to spend time
with others because he enjoys them and they in turn know
that.

4) We must satisfy people's questions.

The apostle Paul is probably talking of more than spiritual warfare when he wrote: "We demolish arguments and every pretension that sets itself up against the knowledge of God . . . " (2 Cor.10:5). There is a sense in which we are called as Christians to clear away the objections that men have about serving the Lord. In the final analysis, no one has any excuse for the rejection of God (Rom. 1:20), and this we will discuss in a later chapter. However, the devil manages to fool some people into thinking that they do have a good reason. We as Christians know that if they were really hungry to do what was right, God would reveal the truth to them (Matt. 7:7-11, Heb 11:6). But, it is still our job to graciously expose that error that blocks their path to God. In all this we need the leading of the Holy Spirit, and also at times, the Holy Spirit's gifts to do a thorough job.

To not be able to answer people's questions satisfactorily, can sometimes serve to confirm them in their unbelief. A man full of honest questions is not always free to share his doubts in a public meeting. Neither does he have the opportunity to ask questions of a television preacher. But, when he is being witnessed to privately it is another matter! Hence the advantage of personal evangelism.

5) Not everybody is able to attend meetings.

Due to social customs and other difficulties related to location—especially in the non-Western World—some people just cannot attend Christian meetings. Others, including some women and many who are handicapped, are confined to the home and will not hear God's message unless someone personally goes to them.

6) Not everybody can watch Christian broadcasts.

As wonderful as the modern mass-communicators are (TV, radio, Christian literature), we still are faced with the fact that they are not meant to make the personal presentation of Christ obsolete. Quite the contrary. My thought is, let's make use of the mass media to carry the gospel message, but let's couple it with the warmth of personal contact.

It is interesting to note that Soviet Christians and other saints in communist countries, have long been denied the privilege of such things as locally based Christian TV and radio programs, city-wide evangelistic rallies, and mass literature crusades. For many years many of these Christians have been denied Bibles. I once heard about a pastor behind the Iron Curtain who had just one page from the Old Testament book of Exodus from which to teach his underground congregation. This continued on for 12 years! Yet even in these lacking-in-media circumstances, our brothers in communist countries have been able to multiply and win others to Christ at an astonishing rate. What then, does God require of us?

We have only to consider the early church to see another example. Although they had rallies, their era was before the advent of the printing press and the invention of both radio and television. Even reduced to the irreducible minimum of mere flesh and blood, the gospel wields phenomenal power through those who show love and concern.

There is no doubting the power of television to communicate the gospel. Millions are being ministered to through this modern mass-communicator. Many are getting saved and healed. Yet as gratifying as all this is, one cannot escape certain realities. Way back in 1970, Haddon Robinson of the International Christian Broadcaster had some interesting facts to report after conducting an extensive survey on those who watched or listened to religious broadcasts on radio and television. His report stated that such religious broadcasts were not reaching the unsaved, but were listened to almost exclusively by Christians.

Unfortunately, despite a phenomenal increase in professionalism in Christian broadcasting, the situation remains very much the same today. In 1984, in a rare cooperative agreement, both evangelists and critics commissioned an extensive study by the University of Pennsylvania's Annenberg School of Communications and the Gallup organization. Their purpose: to determine the impact of the gospel via the medium of television.

According to *TIME* magazine, one of the conclusions of the study was "although the evangelists raise their funds to reach the 'lost,' they mostly reinforce people already committed to evangelical religion." Praise God for all the good that goes on as a result of Gospel TV. It is important to encourage those already saved and reach some of their friends at the same time. But the fact has to be faced that every time certain Christian programs come on the small screen, a great number of sinners switch channels. The University of Pennsylvania survey revealed that *only 6.2% of the American TV audience were regular viewers of the various Christian shows.*[1] A 1985 survey by Nielsen added cable data to the statistics but could only show that a sustantial *minority* of the nation's TV households tune in to Gospel TV for just a few minutes in a week.

Another limitation is this. The latest statistics I have read state that only 10 percent of the homes in the Philippines have a TV set to watch. The percentage, of course, is much higher in Metro-Manila, but the fact remains that there are millions in that nation alone, to say nothing of huge nations like China, India and other Third World countries whose homes will never tune into these broadcasts. They simply don't have the sets to do so and they may never have one.

Even here in America, for the reasons already stated, we cannot expect all to be reached through this media, as wonderful as it is for conveying our message. Let us rejoice at all that God is doing through television. But it does not absolve us, of course, from the responsibility of each of us sharing Christ around us.

7) Not everybody can read Christian literature.

Let's consider another medium of mass-communication, the printed word. It has also been my privilege to have been involved in the writing, publication and distribution of literature. There is no doubting the power of the printed page to attract people's attention, to bring conviction and hope, and to lead people to Christ. K.K. Alavi, for example, was a Moslem from the southern Indian State of Kerala. As a youth, his mind could not escape the truths of God's Word which had been conveyed to him through a booklet he had once bought in a market place where Christians were witnessing. Despite tyrannical persecution from his family, including fierce beatings, God's Word burned into his consciousness and stayed there through the years until he too began to serve the Lord.[2]

Yet even literature has its limitation. In our modern media-oriented world not everybody cares to read. A very low percentage of Filipinos, for example, read books, although they love comics. But that is not the only problem. In the European nation of Portugal only 40 percent of the population can read. In their former colony of Mozambique it is worse. In that country the rate of literacy is only about five per cent. The use of literature, which we should use to the maximum, is severely limited in many low literacy level countries around the world.

Spreading the gospel by means of radio, television, newspapers, books, and magazines are all good ways of presenting Christ. But by themselves, unaided by God's entire army of believers personally presenting the gospel, these ministries as we have just seen, will never ever reach every creature for Christ.

8) If we are to reach the world, everyone must be involved.

The world's population of approximately five billion people is not going to be reached by just a few hundred or even a few thousand evangelists and ministers. Let the following example bring this truth home to us all. Please read the next paragraph slowly and carefully. Brother Andrew wrote the following many years ago but it should still make us stop and think:

> "If from this moment no more people were born in China, and if from now on a revival like that on the day of pentecost took place with 3,000 conversions every day, it would take 725 years before everyone in China was converted. Moreover, 3,000 conversions a day is not very many considering that the population increases by 54,794 every day."[3]

China represents approximately one quarter of the world's population. This should prompt the serious question: "How then, can all the world possibly hear the gospel so Jesus can return?" This question must be faced for Matthew 24:14 reads, "And this gospel of the kingdom will be preached in the whole world as a testimony to all nations, and then the end will come." We know that Christians can actually hasten the day of the Lord from what the apostle Peter wrote: "You ought to live holy and godly lives as you look forward to the day of God and *speed* its coming" (2 Pet. 3:11-12). We can bring back the King, but every Christian needs to be involved.

Let's for a moment consider that the born-again population of the world numbers only two hundred million. That is a very conservative estimate, but it will only serve to strengthen the following illustration. Let's suppose that every one of these born-again believers leads one other person to Christ each year. Let's also assume that the new convert in turn is taught to lead someone else to Christ the following year. At this extremely slow rate of growth, the complete world would be Christian in approximately 12 years. Think of that! If you find this difficult to accept, try working it out with pen and paper. It should be encouraging. One thing that this arithmetical assignment doesn't take into account however, is the imbalanced distribution of Christians throughout the world. But even so, the exercise should give us a clear vision of just how possible Jesus' words are to fulfill when He stated, "Go into all the world and preach the good news . . . " (Mark 16:15).

This should also lead us to ask why we as the church have been so slow to do what our Head has directed. Maybe as an answer we could individually ask ourselves, "How many years have I been a Christian, and how many people have I led to Christ? And how many of these in turn have led others to Jesus?" It is very possible that we have all upset the mathematical equation mentioned above. Even if we pass this test, let us not suppose that the above-stated rate is to be the norm. We could win the world a lot faster if we multiplied ourselves at the rate the church did during the book of Acts. This adds further weight to the fact that world evangelism can be achieved, even within this generation.

9) Personal evangelism is a vital necessity to a well-balanced Christian life.

I can well remember the time in my life when, as a teenager, prayer and Bible reading were not all that exciting to me. Then, as a result of asking God to help me be a Christian influence in High School, the opportunity arose for me to try to witness for the Lord. But I hardly knew what to say to a classmate after a class discussion about religion that day. Witnessing was a brand new experience for me. I said what I could (which wasn't much) and then took him to someone else to do the talking. To my amazement he came to the Lord! And the result of all this? My prayer and Bible reading life was never to be the same after that. I was fired up and arose early each morning to seek the Lord. I now felt responsible to disciple my friend from school and see others in my class come to know the Lord as well. You see, prayer becomes far more meaningful and specific when we are involved in spreading heaven's message in a world of need. And what an encouragement to our prayer-life when there are a number of young converts that we as a group or church have led to the Lord. (That was not to happen as a teenager, but it was to occur later on.) What a thrilling thing to see God answer prayer and deepen their lives! At the same time, the Bible is much more real because it becomes more of a handbook to us. What inspiration the Bible affords to those who are doing the things the disciples of Jesus did.

10) There needs to be a restoration of emphasis on personal evangelism.

If we evangelize personally with the right motive, others will be drawn to follow our example. Many times an aspect of truth becomes almost extinct to Christians in certain localities, not because the Bible is silent on that subject, but because so few Christians are living out that particular facet of God's Word. Personal evangelism *must* be restored to the church all over the world.

We all know how active and successful the early church was in personal evangelism as they scattered over a large area, busily witnessing for Christ. They took the message over to Europe, down into Africa and east into Arabia. Though they were killed by the sword, beheaded, thrown to the lions and even dipped in tar and set alight, they continued to witness. And travel. Tradition says that one of the Lord's disciples, Thomas, was martyred in Madras, South India. Believers must have made it all the way to China at an early date for the Christian concepts to have found their way into the written Chinese language as they did at that time.

However, the church lost its fire. Christianity became an acceptable thing and the church then became more concerned with conferences than they were with outreaches. Finally she sank even further during the Dark Ages. Few were born-again. The clergy kept the Bible to themselves. Witnessing came pretty much to a standstill.

The path back to the church operating as the Lord Jesus desired has been slow but steady. The church everywhere however, must yet be possessed by a passion for witnessing on the personal level. This includes everyone in the body of Christ, despite hardships, privations, persecution and even imprisonment. Denominational barriers must topple and all Christians must work for Christ's kingdom. Will you receive the torch which is beginning to blaze strongly, and then pass it on to others?

---

1.   Time Magazine, February 17, 1986. p. 63.

2.   K.K. Alavi, "In Search of Excellence," G.L.S. Press, Bombay.

3.   Brother Andrew, Open Doors Magazine, 1970.

Chapter Two

HOW TO CONVEY OUR MESSAGE

There is a right way and a wrong way to do everything and this is certainly true in the witnessing situation. Many times people have not responded to our message, simply because of our wrong approach. Sometimes it has been because we have been so negative and condemning. On other occasions, it has not been *what* we said, but *how* we conveyed it. Let's then consider the "do's" and "don'ts" that we should observe when we speak of Christ.

1) We should witness for Christ with enthusiasm.

This is sometimes more easily said than always done. While it is true that witnessing brings its own inherent joy, there are times in the witnessing situation when we feel anything but enthusiastic.

This is where faith needs to be exercised. I like to think that faith is simply doing what God has told us to do, with the right attitude of heart. In the witnessing situation, we have to say to ourselves that we are sharing the message, which God at great cost gave to mankind. We are also obeying the words of our Lord and Master Jesus Christ who commanded us to speak forth for Him (Mark

16:15). Faith also says "After I've obeyed God, I'll leave the circumstances (and my feelings) to Him." Not to be ruled by my feelings, I'm afraid, is a skill I am still learning. I wish that wasn't true but it is. But at the same time, I need to hasten to say that time without number I have done things because God impressed me to do them—even though I did not feel like doing them. Usually in these cases, both the results and my feelings afterwards have been terrific! But not always. I'm still puzzled over some incidents. After obeying the Lord however, faith has to leave the consequences to Him—including those occasions when our feelings are not satisfied.

Witnessing is spiritual warfare and we will be easily discouraged in our witnessing life if we don't understand this concept. The devil has a vested interest in attacking our *feelings* because so many of us are influenced by them. But if we are *not* ruled by our feelings, he'll have a hard time derailing our witnessing efforts. What can we do then, to strengthen our emotional life so our feelings don't drag us down?

The Scriptures tell us: "Submit yourselves then, to God. Resist the devil, and he will *flee* from you. Come near to God and he will come near to you" (James 4:7). According to this verse, the devil will not flee, if we are not submitted to the Lord. In Hebrews 13:15-16 we are then exhorted to take a further step. That passage reads, ". . . let us continually offer to God a sacrifice of praise." This includes praising God for who He is, not for how we may feel. We will find that the devil does not hang around thankful people—nor do feelings of self-pity for that matter. Many of us fail God at this point because the moment the devil gets upset and attacks us with depression and discouragement, we tend to slow down in our work for the Lord.

But just a note of caution. God never approves of falsehood and pretense. Maintaining a positive attitude and endeavoring to rejoice in the Lord when we are conscious of unrepented sin doesn't work very well. If we are aware of wrongdoing in our lives, we need to confess and forsake it. After all, this is what we are asking the unsaved to do. And we can't very well tell non-Christians to do something that we as believers are not doing ourselves. The power of "encouraging ourselves in the Lord" (1 Sam. 30:6), is demonstrated by the following story.

Once, on a door-to-door witnessing crusade in Canada, two young people received a rude reception from a lady whose door they had approached. Still rejoicing however (after all, God is still the same), they made their way back down the path while the woman who rejected them watched from the window. She was struck by the reality which their joyful attitude revealed and she took it all in. Waiting until they had worked their way from house to house down the street and back up the other side, she called them over when they were opposite her house. This time she invited them into her home and after hearing their message, she then proceeded to ask Jesus into her life!

What had attracted her to the Lord? Their doctrine? To some degree perhaps. But mainly I would imagine it was the reality of God in their lives manifested by their joyful attitude. The gospel must be *living* in us, not just words that are printed somewhere in a book. This is not to say that doctrine is unimportant. In fact with some, like Nicodemus of old (John 3), it will be the giving of truth that will "turn them on." But with others, as the story above illustrates, it will be the joy of the Lord in the face of rejection that will speak louder than words. Who knows how much the joy that was on Stephen's face as he was being stoned to death ministered to the hard heart of Saul, the persecutor of the church (Acts 7:54 - 8:1).

The Christian walks a unique pathway because he is linked with God, and has the same power behind him that brought creation into being. The founder of the Christian faith, unlike the founders of every other religion, has risen from the dead. When we witness therefore, we should be aware that the resurrection power of Christ is available to us. It is no credit to Him if we set out to witness as though we do not enjoy it. The pessimist can always find something to grumble about, but the Christian is instructed to be different. The will of God is for him to be thankful, to rejoice in the Lord always and to make melody in his heart to the Lord (Col. 3:16, Phil.4:4, Eph. 5:19).

2) We must use simple terms when we witness.

The importance of speaking to people in language they can understand cannot perhaps, be overemphasized. I think we waste many hours of witnessing because we do not clarify the terms we use. Each profession uses words and expressions almost unintelligible to members of a different profession and unfortunately, we Christians use special terms too.

Let's pause here and ask ourselves if we use the following terms when we witness: personal Savior; moral agent; born again; justified; and saved. The chances are, if we do use them, we will not be getting through to our non-church-going friends. When we communicate we should never give our listeners that "left-out" feeling. That's the feeling you have when the doctor explains you have "dishydrosis" on your hands and a "fistula" somewhere else. One young man here in America, not familiar with "Christianese," read a sign board which announced, "Jesus saves." He honestly thought it meant that Jesus was thrifty with His money!

It is very easy for us to think that because we have spread the gospel, then automatically God's Word will not return to Him void (Is. 55:11). Scripture must balance Scripture however, for Jesus taught that if a man does not *understand* the message of the gospel, then the devil removes those words that we have spoken (Matthew 13:19). God is the greatest communicator and He speaks in ways that others can clearly understand. Our goal therefore, is to present our message as clearly as God does in a simple dynamic way. Then the one listening will at least understand it—even if he chooses to disobey it.

3) We must be friendly.

God strongly desires friendship with man—that is why He made him in the beginning (not because He needed this friendship, but because He wanted to share with man the wonders of His Being). Although later on man's sin deeply grieved Him, it did not alter His desire for continual fellowship with His creatures. God provided a just and loving way to restore that fellowship through the cross. He therefore loves man. But, to hear some folk witness, you would think God is most unfriendly and that He has sent His messengers to torment people! Christians have been guilty of having preached in such a way that the unsaved feel that God is angry with them.

Thus, instead of being attracted to a loving God, people have actually been scared away from the very one who is all-receiving. We must remember that salvation is *knowing* God (John 17:3) and that people will not be inspired to know someone they're afraid of. We must represent God's friendliness and inspire the unsaved to trust His character. To reinforce this concept we must allow people to sense that we are on their level and that we *enjoy* their company.

Although Jesus is the holy Son of God, gamblers, prostitutes and cheats felt loved and understood by Him. Christ befriended these folk—even honoring them. By loving them and spending time in their company, He gave them a chance to change their ways. So must we. In so doing we will help them turn away from their sin. But even if they have no intention of turning to God, we must still continue to love them for their sakes. For too long we as Christians have been guilty of "loving" people for what we can get out of them—a signed decision card or a body in a pew.

Jesus said that God did not send His son into the world to damn the world, but that the world might be rescued through Him (John 3:17). He also taught that in the same way the Father had sent Him, He was now sending us (John 20:21). Jesus therefore sends us today into the world, not to condemn people but that they may be won to Christ through our witness.

We should endeavor to imitate Jesus who witnessed to the woman at the well so naturally that she did not feel that she was being preached to. She certainly did not feel she was being attacked (which is not what many unsaved could say about those who've witnessed to them!) Witnessing should be a friendly, relaxed and natural conversation between two people. It would seem that the only people with whom Jesus spoke sharply were hypocritical spiritual leaders (See Matthew, Chapter 23). To be witnessing to such non-practicing leaders of the way of salvation with hard hearts will be rare. Most people we talk to may have never understood the light of the gospel—especially in many Asian, Latin, Pacific or African locations. Let's be patient with them. Remember, we also were in darkness once, and during that time we justified our sinful actions.

In his book, *Taking Men Alive,* Charles Trumbull maintains that we can discover in any person at least one thing we can approve of. He goes on to describe the time when a drunkard staggered cursing and swearing into the same train car as the one in which he was traveling. It probably wasn't just the train that was swaying as the drunkard walked down the aisle. Lurching into the seat beside Mr. Trumbull, the drunk offered a drink from his flask. Inwardly, Trumbull drew back from the foul-mouthed man. However, instead of showing rejection and disdain, Trumbull responded with, "No thank you, but I see you are very generous." The man's eyes lit up in appreciation and the two began to talk. The drunk was deeply touched. Like those to whom Jesus spoke personally, this drunken man relaxed his defenses in this environment of acceptance and subsequently came to the Lord. But how many of us would have thrown away the opportunity to win this man to Christ by being busy in a ministry of condemnation. If we want to attract folk to Christ, let's approve where we can.

When speaking about man's sin, as we must, remember that this is an area where people are usually very sensitive. Speak in such a way that those listening to you will feel they could trust you with the worst possible information about their sin—and still be cared for. This does not mean to say we are to excuse sin and say it cannot be avoided. Otherwise there would be no need for a conscience and no need to live in accordance with the standards laid down in the Bible. But on the other hand, let's not "rub it in" by our attitude of harshness or self-righteousness. People are basically proud and do not easily acknowledge their sinful state. We only make it harder for them to admit their sin if we use condemning language. After all, none of us likes to be scolded. And if we remember that we as Christians often fail God, we will be more likely to speak with compassion. People will more readily respond to our call to repentance if they sense we accept and enjoy them. This is the example that Jesus gave us through His personal witnessing experiences as described in the four gospels.

Whatever you do, always leave the unsaved in such a way that they will readily welcome another Christian into his life. That other Christian will then take them one step closer to the Lord until finally someone will be able to lead them to faith. Do not try to rush people into salvation. True conversion represents a total change of life-style. It is turning from everything we know is wrong; it is the rejection of selfish living and the giving of ourselves in love to God. We cannot always expect a person to make this huge decision the first time he hears about this new way of life. You probably had a number of contacts with Christians, or with experiences through which God spoke, before you finally yielded your life to Him. Some of us had years of exposure to Sunday School and church or to a Christian family. Therefore, we should be content to lead our friend along the path that leads to salvation just as far as he is ready to go. Then let the next Christian take him further.

4) We should be good listeners.

When we witness we cannot afford to be impatient or give

the appearance that we are bursting to be able to say something if only they would just keep quiet! That kind of attitude of course, will not minister to them. As a general rule it is good to let a person say what he wants to—within reason. To interrupt him or her can be a mistake, because they will feel they are unimportant and that you don't care about them. In my view, it was giving sinners the feeling that they were accepted that was a major key to Jesus' success in personal evangelism. Listening sympathetically will minister that feeling of acceptance. The need that there is for a listening ear is illustrated by the following story.

Before setting out on a Greyhound bus from Los Angeles to Northern California one summer, I prayed that God would place beside me the person He wanted me to witness to. As the bus hissed and started out on the long journey, the seat beside me remained empty. About half way through the trip, however, there was a commotion at the back of the bus and an old woman cursing and muttering to herself came from behind and plunked herself in that empty seat beside me. Looking at her face, I caught myself thinking how embittered she appeared. Her face looked so hard! I remember thinking, *Someone in her life has really hurt her.* This became apparent as we engaged in conversation. She almost spat out, "I have buried one husband and divorced the other," as a result of their drinking habits. The commotion at the back of the bus had been caused by her repulsion to a drunkard there, who had triggered the memory of her past husbands. Unfortunately she had allowed her hurt to turn into hardness which was evident just by looking at her.

She began to talk and I listened. Continuing through the Central Californian landscape to the sound of the hum of the bus' wheels on the hot roads, she continued to talk and I continued to listen. Finally she wondered aloud, "Why am I sharing these things with you?" Then in answer to her own question she thoughtfully said, "I know. It's because people today don't listen anymore!"

Sympathetic listening had done wonders for her. I was

amazed. Her face, once so hard, had softened dramatically. Suddenly I noticed I was sitting beside a very likeable old lady!

If you have a desire to listen, you will find you'll grow in compassion. And with compassion you'll inspire people to open up to you as you witness. Listening compassionately is the opposite to arguing. We are not listening when we argue because we are so intent on getting our view across. Arguing demeans. It says "My view and I are more important than what you think. I do not respect your opinion; therefore I do not respect you." But if we listen we are saying "I do respect you." And that is just what the sinner needs to sense from us.

The reason the world needs Christians to respect and love them is this. Self-esteem is a commodity without which no human being can live. Jesus acknowledged our need for it when He said that we were to love our neighbors as *ourselves* (Matt. 22:39), and the apostle Paul assumed the right kind of self-love was legitimate when he wrote, "After all no one ever hated his own body, but feeds and cares for it . . ." (Eph. 5:29). But self-esteem is very scarce today, especially when the emphasis is so much on beauty, money and position. The average person just can't compete in this "winner-take-all" world. But we Christians, of all people, have it in our power to compassionately listen in such a way as to nourish this vital commodity and thus draw people to the Savior. In a book written many years ago, Dorothy Walter Baruch mentioned the things everybody needs in order to function in emotional strength, regardless of age. The most important two things, she wrote, are acceptance and understanding.[1] I believe these are nourished through listening.

Listening compassionately creates the very atmosphere that we all need so much. If anyone in the world can show the way to a healthy self-image it should be Christians. The ultimate way of course, is through fellowship with the living Christ, but the unsaved don't have this resource until they are converted. Nevertheless, the way we treat the non-Christian (as well as the Christian) can still minister acceptance or rejection. Even when we answer a question we should do it carefully. Do not sigh as if to say that you have answered that particular question a hundred times before, even though that might be true. Maintain a fresh and original approach.

One last comment on this subject. You will find that non-Westerners are extremely interaction-oriented (as we mentioned in the *Before We Begin* section of this book). This makes the need to listen even more imperative. They will much more readily respond to us if we do.

5) We should witness with boldness.

I was once very afraid to open my mouth for Jesus to some people. The thought that plagued me was that they would think me "strange" or look at me sideways. Then there were certain individuals I was actually terrified to say anything to.

Yet one of the most oft-repeated commandments in the Bible is the injunction, "Fear not!" Much of my fear was caused by sheer unbelief, which the Bible calls sin (Heb. 3:12). This is because in effect I was saying, "God won't look after me." Fear was also the result of pride because I was afraid of what people would say or think about me. That's still something I have to face today.

But with experience I began to think that it is the non-Christian who should feel strange—not me. This is because I belong to the King of the universe and am simply doing what He has instructed. As the boldness slowly increased, I began to realize that I was simply acting out a Scripture I had read years earlier. It told me that when I am not frightened it's a sign to the unbeliever that I am from God and that it is they who are on the path to destruction (Phil.1:28).

Boldness then, is the ability to look people in the eye with a quiet authority and speak the message of Christ in love. In fact, the more love we have, the more bold we can be. Love is so unthreatening. When people are convinced

we love and care for them it's amazing how much correction they will receive from us. That's not to say it will always work like that. We have to be prepared for our words
to be opposed or politely ignored. But in non-Western
countries, the chances of our words being received are
much higher if we witness in a loving way—even if we are
saying things they would rather not hear. On the other
hand, the chances of our being heard are just about nil
when we are harsh and rude.

The best cure for nervousness of course, is the power
of the Holy Spirit. Christ never intended that His disciples
should go out to witness without first receiving the power
of the Spirit-filled life (Acts 1:8, Eph. 5:18). Neither did He
intend us to approach the unsaved biting our fingernails.
How we need to be Spirit-filled today.

Derek Prince once said in an address that if we take
the words like speak, preach, talk, and witness as found in
the book of Acts, we will find that they occur over one
hundred times in reference to Christians sharing about
Jesus Christ and His gospel. We may do little preaching,
Prince concludes; nevertheless, our purpose as Christians
is to open our mouths about the Lord Jesus everywhere we
go.

It is the power of the Holy Spirit that gives us this
freedom to speak (Acts 2:4, 8:17, 10:44-48, 9:17, 19:6). It is
this experience and the continual infilling of the Holy
Spirit that keeps us witnessing.

I have found that the more I witness the easier it becomes. And if I don't witness for a while, then the fear of
man can come creeping back. But not entirely, for the experience of the infilling of the Holy Spirit and His love,
plus the confidence I have learned from witnessing in the
past can all be resummoned. Let's then persevere, so that
fear would lessen and that through experience we would
learn to be effective. Each Christian has the responsibility
to become an effective witness. So don't give up. You just
keep right on giving that witness for the Lord!

1. Dorothy Baruch, "New Ways in Discipline," "You and Your Child Today," (New York, McGraw-Hill Book Company).

Chapter Three

THE NECESSITY OF PRAYER

Prayer has such an important role to play in the economy of God. The gospels for example, record Jesus' long hours of prayer either at a time long before daybreak or in a solitary place during the night hours (Mark 1:35; Luke 5:16; 6:12). The Bible as a whole reveals prayer preceded major events in the plan of God. Moses, for example, spent six weeks alone with God on the mountain before the giving of the Ten Commandments, and Jesus spent forty days in the wilderness praying and fasting before the commencement of His earthly ministry. Later his disciples were in the place of prayer before the outpouring of God's power on the day of Pentecost.

When it comes to evangelism, there seems to be a direct relationship between the amount of effort spent in prayer and being effective. I well remember the time in the early 1970's when Margaret and I were leading a team that traveled through some Asian countries for one year. During our stay in a sophisticated area of Bangkok, Thailand, our team was finding it very hard to get through to people. Many are aware of the evil spiritual powers that hover over that country. We were witnessing in the afternoons, and that week we had three scheduled meetings to which those we had contacted during the day were invited. Our first evening meeting was poorly attended. As a team we decided to fast and pray and stopped witnessing for the day. At the meeting that night, the attendance was no better. If anything it was even worse! But when we went out to witness next we sensed the difference and the meeting that night was so much better. It was attended by more people and also the presence of God was there. We must have a heart to both pray and witness. The two go together.

The trip around Asia mentioned above, ended with the team and Margaret and I working in the southern Philippine City of Davao, on the Island of Mindanao. One day Margaret was impressed in her daily reading with a verse from Isaiah which says, in part, "You who call on the Lord, give yourselves no rest, and give him no rest till he establishes Jerusalem" (Is. 62:6-7). Accordingly, for two months, the eight of us on that team maintained an around-the-clock prayer vigil as we prayed for the nation, its government, for Davao and for our ministry in that city. We were to see before long the conversion of some young people, who have just been a joy to us. Writing now some 16 years later, I am happy to say that a nucleus of those who came to the Lord that year have been involved in full-time Christian work and are good Christians today. Later we were to witness the ushering in of a decade of peace and stability in the nation, from the chaos and anarchy that was then in existence (in 1972).

We returned to Davao in 1987 many years after the events described above had taken place. At the time of our return we had 16 adults with us from an evangelism course that we had led in Hawaii at YWAM's Pacific & Asia Christian University (PACU). Many on the U.S. mainland were praying for us and much prayer went up during the lecture phase of the course in Hawaii. During the official three-month outreach time of this PACU course in Davao, a lot of prayer went on—some of it for the establishment of the first-ever YWAM Discipleship Training School (DTS) to be held in the south of the Philippines. The local Ywammers led by Graeme Jones were praying too.

The result was that God drew outstanding students

(almost all Filipinos) to that school who were eager to learn, serve God and pray. In the classroom God moved among them in confession, openness and with His cleansing power. When it came time to go out on outreach they took with them what God had done in their lives in the school. As a result, Christians in far flung places of the South of the Philippines were both revived and refreshed. Church members openly got right with the Lord and with one another as these students preached, testified and shared what they had learned in the DTS.

A study of moves of God's Spirit through history, where large numbers of people have been converted, will reveal that travailing prayer preceded these events. Perhaps the most widely known move of the Spirit was the Welsh Revival of 1904 in which 100,000 people obeyed God in repentance and entered the kingdom of God in a short space of time. The person most identified with this revival was a young man of 26 years called Evan Roberts who was studying for the ministry. For 13 months before the revival came, he had been praying for the Spirit to sweep the land. Other intercessors were also praying when the revival broke out, but Evan had been praying so hard he had been asked to leave his place of lodging. He had spent so many hours praying and preaching in his bedroom that his landlady became afraid and asked him to leave! [1]

Another example of revival occurring as the result of intercession is the case of the marvelous occurrences that took place in the Islands of the Hebrides off the coast of Scotland in 1949. This move of God saw thousands swept into His kingdom in just a matter of months. Even drunkards called out to God for mercy in the street. One night young people fled from a dance hall to plead God's mercy in a neighboring church at two o'clock in the morning. The genesis of these glorious happenings were prayer meetings that lasted through the night.

But there is an important aspect of prayer for evangelism and revival that often gets overlooked by Christians. It is the aspect of Christians breaking over their sins. This is the principle so clearly stated to King Solomon after he had asked God for wisdom regarding being the leader over Israel. In Second Chronicles the Lord shared with his servant that if God sent a drought or another calamity, then it was up to the people of God to do something about it. It was not the labor Unions, or the Communists or the Government but *God's people* who had to pray and humble themselves. They also had to turn from all that they knew was wrong. In the case of the Revival in the Hebrides just mentioned, Christians cried out to God for the removal of the spiritual drought over the land by meeting in a barn twice a week and praying through the night. But it was not until they began confessing their sin that God moved in power. The Lord was justly able to send His conviction upon the unsaved because Christians had humbled themselves first.

Let's look at just one more example of how prayer influences revival. In the year 1857, Jeremiah Lamphier gave up his business and walked the streets of downtown New York advertising a noonday prayer meeting to be held in a centrally located church the next Wednesday. The result? Six men finally showed up half an hour late. But on the following Wednesday, twenty people were in attendance. Six months later over 10,000 businessmen met *daily* in similar prayer meetings. They confessed their sin, they came to Christ and they prayed for revival. They met in stores, in churches and in company offices. In just two years over a million souls came to Christ. The blessing spread across the Atlantic to Ireland and Great Britain. During this time the ministries of such people as D. L. Moody, Ira Sankey, William and Catherine Booth (The Salvation Army) and Hudson Taylor (China Inland Mission) were developed that were to have far reaching effects in other places around the globe. [2]

So we are as effective in evangelism as we are effective in prayer. Prayer of course, means more than intercession. It also means fellowship with God where we learn of His character. If the level of our communion with God is low, so too will our effectiveness be low in communicating Christ. It is only to the extent that we know God's love and presence that we will be able to share what God is like, and it is the character of God we really need to exhibit to a hurting world. If God is speaking to us in prayer, and we are enjoying friendship with Him, then our lives will more readily reflect the life of Christ. This in turn will be more noticed by the sinner who will thus respond much faster to what we say. Making God known is a natural outcome of knowing God. Thus, to be effective, we must grow to know God more and more.

History doesn't indicate we are always in revival (although one outstanding revivalist of the 1800's— Charles Finney—believed it was ours for the asking). This does not mean we do nothing in the realm of evangelism in the meantime. We still need to witness. And pray as we witness. For what then, should we pray? In addition to allowing God to show us our hearts (so we can repent from anything He shows us), we should pray that we be filled anew with the Spirit. We need to pray that God will lead us to the right people; both those whose attention we will turn to spiritual matters for the first time, and those who will be ready to obey the Lord in repentance and thus begin a love relationship with Him.

On our YWAM crusades it is normal that we go out two by two in the manner described in Luke 10:1 and Acts 13:2. With each contact, one should be praying while the other is talking. This praying partner has a very important job to do because his prayers can affect the course of the conversation. It is his job to pray against the many disturbances that can occur. Remember, witnessing includes combating the enemy who can use children crying, telephones ringing and a number of other things to keep people from even hearing our word. The praying partner should be praying that the Holy Spirit would convince people of God's tender love, and yet at the same time convict them of the awfulness of their sin.

Many times it is important that both the silent partner and the one doing the speaking should at appropriate times persistently come against Satan who has blinded so many people to the truths of the gospel (2 Cor. 4:4). How wonderful it is to see Satan submit when we persistently resist him in Jesus' mighty name! Many times it is the devil who influences men to have unbelief, hatred or to be worried about the opposition they might receive from relatives if they become Christians.

But our praying does not stop when we stop talking. It is possible that the period immediately following a time out witnessing is when we can be more effective in prayer. This is because the Holy Spirit has words to use—words that you and I have spoken. He will also remind them of your example of godliness, joy and peace—the fragrance of Christ demonstrated in your life.

The importance of prayer will again be dealt with in a later chapter when we discuss the subject of follow-up, for the apostle Paul constantly prayed for those to whom he preached and among whom he labored (Eph.1:16-18, 1 Thess 1:2-3, 2 Tim 1:3-4). I trust enough about prayer has been discussed in this chapter to make us all hungry to pray.

---

1.   Winkie Pratney, "Revival," (Springdale, PA Whitaker House, 1983), p. 175.
2.   ibid p. 144-146.

Chapter Four

GIVING A TESTIMONY

N ow we come to another important part of our Christian witness—telling others of our own personal experience with the Lord Jesus. As we witness for Christ, it is likely that we will meet people who will refuse to recognize the truth of the doctrines that we present. And it is here that we have a vital and powerful weapon that no person can deny. Because of this we have included this guideline for you to use when you give your testimony.

1) Let's witness to Christ.

Acts 1:8 tells us that we shall be witnesses to *Him*. This means that our testimony will be God-centered and not a testimony to our church or even a plan of salvation. It is important that we indicate that we are talking about a *person* and how it is possible to be lovingly related to Him.

2) Let's be relevant.

While small talk is very often legitimate, the thrust of our witnessing should deal with our conversion and life in Christ. The people we witness to may very well be interested in knowing about the events leading to our being at the location where we were converted. But let's make sure they realize our emphasis is the change that Christ has made in our lives!

3) Let's be specific.

If we speak in general terms and say things like, "Christ has changed my life so wonderfully," it will not be as meaningful as it would be if we were to mention exactly what God has changed in our lives. It is better therefore, to mention those things that Jesus has delivered us from, like guilt, worry, fear and so on. These are real problems in people's lives today and they will easily relate to these. As we tell them how Christ changed our lives in specific areas, they will realize that He can change their lives in those same areas too. They will probably be inspired to trust him in other areas as well.

Christianity is an inward change of heart and this is what we must always express. It does more good, I think, if we tell others how Christ has helped us overcome feelings of revenge, lust or pride that were in our lives than to tell them that we don't go the bars, wild parties and X-rated movies any more.

4) Let's make our testimonies up-to-date.

We must be communing with the Lord and having a daily experience of His overcoming power in our lives before we can witness effectively. Let's not just tell how Christ has changed our lives or spoken to us in the past. Let's also testify to how He is changing our lives and speaking to us *today*.

5) Let's be truthful.

Jesus taught that the Holy Spirit is the Spirit of Truth (John 16:13). Because of this, the endorsement of the Holy

Spirit, which is absolutely essential if our witness is to be effective, cannot come upon our words unless what we say is true. The temptation might come to some, "If I were to exaggerate just a little, then my testimony will sound more impressive!" Don't do it, for the opposite is the truth. When we don't tell the truth, the Holy Spirit cannot endorse our words. So remember, no exaggerating!

6) People love hearing honest stories about us.

Once I listened to a speaker expand on the differences between the kingdom of God and the kingdom of Satan. It was a very good message, but I noticed that the audience became the quietest and the most receptive when the speaker mentioned about the time in his life when he was filled with fear. He told the story of what it was like to be dominated by this fear as he traveled as a fix-it man for a large firm. First of all he was afraid of flying, but then he was also filled with worry that he wouldn't be able to do what his firm wanted him to do. The night before he would fly away on business he would toss and turn despite the comfort of his hotel bed.

He had the attention of us all as he told that story. The reason I believe was three-fold. Firstly, people love stories. Secondly, he was speaking from a low position— not a haughty one, and thirdly, we all identified with him as he told us about a weakness that had been in his life. We all have those. Try therefore, to tell your testimony like that. You'll more readily have people's attention if you do.

As a final practical step to aid you in giving a truthful, relevant and specific testimony, write out your testimony as though you were giving it to a non-Christian. Bear in mind all the points mentioned here and the earlier exhortation not to use church jargon like "redeemed" and "personal Savior." Write down at least two specific examples of how Christ has changed your life. Happy testifying!

Chapter Five

HOW TO OPEN THE CONVERSATION

In order to reach people for Christ during the everyday activities of life, we need to have some understanding of how to turn the conversation from the mundane to the things of God. With experience, this can be done very simply and effectively. In the incident with the women at the well, Jesus spoke of spiritual matters so naturally that the woman hardly knew that He was witnessing to her. Some people will stiffen and begin to resist our message the moment they feel we are trying to "convert" them, so a natural entrance into witnessing is needed with this kind of person.

This is not to say that gently turning the conversation from day-to-day topics to a spiritual topic is the only way to present Christ. Obviously the Greeks knew what the apostle Paul was going to speak about on Mars Hill (Acts 17). But with a lot of people, a more indirect approach is needed. I trust the following examples will shed light on what it means to turn an everyday conversation into an opportunity to witness for the Lord.

Late one Sunday night I placed a long-distance call to a friend through the operator. The phone at my friend's home rang and rang, so finally the operator suggested that because there was no reply, my friend must be at a party. I could have easily said, "Thank you very much for trying," and hung up. But I sensed that this would be an opportunity to use for the Lord, so I replied: "No, she won't be at a party. She will probably be at church." I knew that this would stir some interest, as most people would not still be at church because of the lateness of the hour.

"At church! What church?" came the inquiry from the other end of the line. I told her, and then asked her as casually as I could, "Are you interested in Christian things?"

The reply was not overwhelmingly positive, so I asked her as naturally as I could, why she felt that way. On and on went the conversation, until about fifteen minutes later, it was I, not she, who ended the conversation. But not before an address was obtained so I could send her some literature. I also invited her to talk further with Margaret and me over dinner. Although she didn't accept that invitation, it is an indication of how well the conversation had gone for me to even suggest that. And remember, being an operator on duty, she could have easily cut me off at any point. But she obviously had become interested in what we were discussing.

I can well remember on another occasion going to the shoe repairman just up the street from the house in Auckland, New Zealand where we lived many years ago when we directed YWAM in that country. It was the inner city, so consequently it was a busy part of town. I entered the tiny customer part of the store and stood waiting to be attended. Soon a man, complete with a shoe repairman's apron, was handing me my shoes. As he did so he said, "I am not likely to see you again because I've done such a good job on your shoes. They'll need no further repairing!"

Once more I could have said, "Thank you very much," paid him the money and left the store. But I sensed this was another opportunity for me to witness. Little did he know that I was in charge of a witnessing program at that time which saw young people go from house to house for a week at a time. In a natural way, I told him how much walking I did and explained the program. Then, as informally as I could, I asked, "Are you interested in these things?"

The conversation began. Another customer came into that little waiting area, retreating as he did so from the noise and bustle of the busy sidewalk just a mere few feet away. It seemed to make no difference to the shoe repairman that another customer was now waiting. So we continued to talk. Feeling sorry for the poor guy waiting to be served, it was I who finally ended the conversation and then continued it the next time I saw the repairman.

I could continue to give examples of conversations opened with store-keepers, gas station attendants and fellow travelers. But I trust my point is made. People will listen to us if our approach is natural and friendly. And, in those countries where prevailing concepts or religions have prejudiced the minds of people against our Lord Jesus, a more indirect and friendly approach is even more necessary. If we feel embarrassed however, they will too. But if we feel friendly and natural, they will feel at ease. After all, Christianity is the norm as far as God is concerned. So why shouldn't we feel confident?

I am convinced that organized evangelical outreaches *alone* are not going to get our job done. The only way I can see all the world hearing the message of Christ is by every Christian being involved in person-to-person evangelism in addition to that which is organized by churches and mission groups. Opportunities can be made if they don't make themselves. But these opportunities can not always be made or taken if we are more intent upon living for material comforts than for God. Jesus warned that the cares of the world, the deceitfulness of riches, and the lust of other things will choke our testimony for Christ (Mark 4:19). Witnessing involves spending time with people which may necessitate passing up the chance for extra sales next weekend or may mean saying "no thank you" the next time the boss gives an opportunity to work overtime.

Witnessing is also work. Perhaps this is why, in our huffing and puffing societies, we don't spend as much time in witnessing as we should. So taken up with the world of "getting on" and "keeping up" with the neighbors, we have little time or energy for sharing Christ. This of course, should not be the case.

But then some of us don't like work—period, and this is possible why more time is not spent in witnessing. This is not to say that we are to neglect our God-given responsibilities to our homes, parents and families. And if we happen to be married, our wives and children are our first responsibility. But regardless of what our commitments are in life, to know God and make Him known should still be our consuming desire.

But what about those times of witnessing in an organized way, like being part of some church-sponsored witnessing drive? How do we open the conversation during those times? In this kind of situation we are obviously not making contact with people for any other reason than to preach Christ. In the examples just given, there were reasons *besides* the gospel that brought me in contact with people. I used these as a natural lead into a spiritual conversation.

Even at the door, or in the park, street, jail or hospital we should at least act naturally and believe that we have the right to be doing what we are doing. And we should be gentle and friendly in our approach. This will always go a long way to endear us to those we are contacting. If we can think of some natural comment about the weather, or a friendly remark about the children, or some appropriate statement about the surroundings, we should offer this. Jesus did. He asked the woman at the well for a drink and then began witnessing to her.

It is also normal to introduce yourself, the name of your church or organization (if you're in a culture that is friendly to Christianity) and the most unoffensive reason for doing what you are doing. An introduction like the following is often possible:

> "Good morning. My name is John and this
> is my friend, Jim. We are two young men
> who want to tell you something very impor-

tant. We would like to tell you how our lives
have been completely changed. You see
two years ago, I . . . . "

You'll find that kind of approach very acceptable,
especially in the Third World. And, in that area of the
world, it is usual to be invited inside to talk. Use this advantage. People are more likely to respond to you in the
privacy of their own home. So, if you find people who are
interested to talk, you may even feel the freedom to politely ask if you could come in and share.

Many times in Asian cultures however, to mention
Christ or His church in the first sentence, is to invite a cold
reception. If people do not know anything about Jesus, we
are wise to follow the biblical pattern and introduce the
concept of God first. It took the Godhead at least four
thousand years to prepare humanity for the advent of
Christ. We too, need to lay a foundation before introducing Jesus Christ in our witnessing conversation.

In Thailand, we once used a technique which effectively got us involved in conversation with the inhabitants
of the housing block where we were witnessing. (This approach will work in a friendly, talkative society. I'd be
hesitant to do it in a cynical or critical one. They could
quite easily be offended.) The Bangkok missionaries, with
whom we were working, had prepared a list of questions
which we presented at each door as part of a religious census. Besides asking them their religion, which was usually
Buddhist, we would ask them their occupation and relevant
details. After recording this information, we would ask if
they had ever studied any other religion and come to any
conclusion about the beginning of the world. There was a
real point to this question, because a pure Buddhist (as opposed to a Chinese Buddhist who is more of an ancestral
worshipper) does not believe God created the world. Using
our Thai partner as an interpreter, we would normally get
involved in a conversation as a result of this approach.

Sometimes when we ask people if they are interested
in talking, they will answer in the negative. At this point we

need to be sensitive to the Spirit. Sometimes we should respect that, and perhaps just leave them with a tract if they care to take one. At other times however, you may feel to thoughtfully and slowly say, "Oh, is there some particular reason why you are not interested?" This can actually lead them into giving you the objection they have to the gospel—an objection to which you may well be able to respond. Actually, they may be very interested in hearing your reply. There have been occasions when I have said something like, "Aren't you interested in a loving God who cares about you?" That question, asked in a kind way, has kept the conversation going. But, even so, be careful not to be obnoxious. God has given people free-will which means the freedom to say "No. I don't want to listen to you." The important thing is to know when to be friendly (and sensitively pursue the conversation) and when to back off immediately.

We should also be careful not to force a tract on someone who doesn't want it. It could be they'll accept a tract from a Christian in the future because we've respected their sovereignty this time. Remember, it is always better to leave the path open for the next Christian to witness than for us to leave them with a bad taste in their mouths.

On the other hand, I think we occasionally miss opportunities that can lead to conversions. Who knows what may have been the outcome of the life of the banker from Sri Lanka if I had not asked to see him again?

So much then for opening the conversation. What do we say after that . . . ?

II. PRESENTING THE MESSAGE

Chapter Six

A PATTERN TO FOLLOW

We now want to discuss what to say to our unsaved friends once we have opened the conversation. As we turn to the Word of God and look at the example of the apostle Paul, we make an interesting discovery. He had two very different approaches, depending on whether the audience was made up of Jews or Gentiles. This holds a lot of significance for us today.

To more readily understand the first of these two different approaches, let's pretend that we are Jewish, and we're sitting in a synagogue in the City of Antioch. It's the very day that Paul and Barnabas are in attendance. We've heard about this Rabbi Saul (now known as Paul) who grew up under the teaching of the famed Rabbinical Lecturer in Jerusalem called Gamaliel. The elders of the synagogue have asked Paul to speak in acknowledgement that he must have something important to say. He is now on the dais in the center of the synagogue saying things we have long heard and cherished. He is both recounting Israeli history and quoting from Scripture. Now he is talking about the promised Messiah. Yes, we've heard so much about our coming Deliverer ever since we could remember. We expect Him to come some day. But, what's this? He is linking the Scriptures which talk about someone who has already come! He is saying that the life, death and resurrection of a miracle-worker in Galilee called Jesus fulfills Messianic promises. He is speaking so convincingly. The events in Jesus of Nazareth's life certainly fulfill so many of our Messianic expectations. My, this is astounding!

The important aspect of the above "pretending exercise" is this: Although the apostle was introducing a brand new concept (Jesus is the promised Messiah), he did it in a way that the hearer could more readily accept. He used concepts with which the hearers were already familiar and then moved logically to bring them to an understanding of the concepts that were new to them.

Now let's look at the time the apostle was in Lystra as an example of his other approach—the one he used when he talked to unsaved Gentiles. Soon after his time in the synagogue just mentioned (Acts 13), Paul and Barnabas traveled along the road to Lystra, a city that was a part of the Roman Province of Galatia. The patron god of this city was *Zeus*, the supreme ruler of men in Greek mythology. (Zeus, whose temple was located outside the city had powers similar to the Roman God, Jupiter.) The Greeks had come to regard Zeus as the only god who was concerned with the whole universe.

Despite it being a heathen city, it didn't take long for the apostles to gather a crowd and begin to preach. While Paul was holding forth in this way, a crippled man who had never walked, listened carefully. Sensitive to the Holy Spirit, the apostle "saw that he had faith to be healed and called out, 'Stand up on your feet!' " (Acts 14:9-10). At his command, the cripple leaped into action and began walking. The crowd went wild!

Their enthusiasm was understandable. After all, how often did a miracle like that happen? Their excitement however, was also misguided for the following reason.

According to an ancient legend, Zeus and another Greek god called *Hermes* ("the messenger of the gods"—a rough equivalent of the Roman god Mercury) were supposed to have visited the same general geographical area in which Paul and Barnabas now found themselves. According to this legend, Zeus and Hermes had not been recognized by anyone except an elderly couple. The people of Lystra therefore were determined not to allow such an oversight to occur again![1] Perhaps this explains what happened next: They began shouting out in the local dialect, "The gods have come down to us in human form!" (verse 11). They named Barnabas, Zeus (perhaps he was the more imposing figure), and Paul they named Hermes because he was the chief speaker. The legend just referred to may explain why the priest of the temple of Zeus brought bulls and wreaths, and why he and the crowd wanted to offer sacrifices to the apostles. It's against this background then, that we look at the section of Paul's message in this town that is recorded in the book of Acts—the time when Paul and Barnabas stopped the crowds from offering sacrifices to them.

Paul began with the concept of God (verse 15), yet even here he did not assume that they knew who God was, because they had already considered Paul and Barnabas to be gods due to the miraculous healing of the crippled man. Consequently, he felt it necessary to explain just what he meant by this term "God." He taught two things: that God was the Creator (verse 15), and that He was good in character because he sent them rain, good crops, food and gladness (verse 17).

To put it simply, Paul mentioned those things with which his hearers were familiar (rain, good crops, food and gladness), and moved from there. He taught new precepts by building upon concepts that they already held. *Let's call this the principle of finding common ground.* Although his intended sermon is cut short due to opposition from a third party, enough of his address is recorded to know how sensitively he started. The approach Paul used would not be too unlike the approach we should make today when communicating to tribal people who are animists anywhere in the world.

"Fine," you might say. "So I've learned that Paul found common ground among the Jews and the heathen and then moved from there. But that doesn't mean two different approaches." A closer look will reveal something however, that is all important to us as we evangelize both in the Western and non-Western Worlds. What makes the difference in the two approaches is *the attitude on the part of the hearer to the Word of God in each instance.* Paul used the Scriptures as a basis for his argument with those who were conversant with them and who believed in them. But he didn't use the Scriptures with those who were not familiar with them. This is a second important principle.

Although the apostle didn't quote Scriptures in Lystra, he nevertheless preached the *truth* of the Word of God in terms that they could relate to. In other words, by using simple illustrations that they could understand (rain, good crops, and so on), he got the Word of God across to them without actually quoting it to them. After all, there is little point in saying, "Thus saith Moses," when they had never heard of the Bible.

The two illustrations, drawn from Scripture we have looked at, are not isolated incidents in the history of the church as recorded in the Book of Acts. The apostle Peter, for example, quoted freely from the Scriptures on the day of Pentecost (Acts 3:12-26). Again, the hearers on that occasion were also conversant with them for they were Jews or Jewish converts who had come in from all over. But the apostle Paul used the other approach when he met with the educated Greeks on Mars Hill (Acts 17:22-34). There in Athens, Paul not only pointed to creation to back up his statements but also quoted from the works of well-known Greek poets (sometimes called prophets) who had written things in accordance with the Word of God (verses 27-28). The Spirit of God evidently approved of this sermon because some joined Paul afterwards and became believers (verse 34).

It should be noted that in dealing with those not familiar with the Scriptures, Paul sought to establish first of all the existence and goodness of God. He did this by saying that his hearers should not worship men but turn to the living God who made heaven and earth, and who is good in that He gave mankind fruitful seasons and satisfied man's heart with food and gladness (Acts 14:15-17).

He then proceeded to bring his hearers into accountability by announcing that God requires all men everywhere to repent. In other words, he was contrasting the overwhelming goodness of God with man's sinfulness. His next step was to introduce Christ as the only way to salvation, which he did on Mars Hill (Acts 17:30- 31).

Let's also discover another principle. We know that all Paul lived for was Christ (Phil. 1:21). Yet despite this, he did not mention the Savior during this discourse in Lystra. Naturally, if he had been allowed to continue his message, he certainly would have preached Christ as there is salvation in no other (Acts 4:12). In the part of the sermon that is recorded for us here, Paul could not have mentioned the concept of Jesus, the Savior of the world, because there was no foundation of understanding in their mind to do that. This introduces us to another principle: *There is a logical and correct time to introduce new concepts, even the concept that Jesus is the son of God.* We cannot talk about the character of God until we have established belief in a Supreme Being. And we cannot introduce the concept of a Savior without laying the foundation of a belief in a good God and the sinfulness of man.

Moslems believe in God, but their concept of Him is not the same as that which we read of in the New Testament. To them, Allah is not a loving tender Father but an aloof omnipotent Being whose emphasis is on judgment. They believe He has predestined their lives so there is no sense in trying to change them. They also believe in sensual rewards for those who die while converting people to Islam via the sword. Thus, time has to be spent with them in the area of our common ground (e.g. the existence of God). But from there it would be wise to enter a conversation that would help them understand something of God's character—both of His love and holiness. Friendship evangelism is very important here. So is sharing our testimony about how God leads us day by day (leaving out mention of Jesus for a while). This is a powerful way to get involved in a witnessing conversation with a Moslem.

Some time ago I used this method as I talked for quite a while to a national of the country of Kuwait while waiting for a delayed flight at Colombo airport in Sri Lanka. (Praise the Lord that delays give us witnessing opportunities!) Later on board the Air Lanka flight, Kuhammed left his own allocated seat and sat down beside me. We talked some more about the things of God. Finally, his curiosity was fully aroused. He jabbed his hand forward and asked in his broken English, "How can I get close to the God?" It was at that point I began carefully introducing the concept of Jesus Christ being God's son (the hardest of all Christian concepts for a Moslem to accept). Kuhammed raised no argument, but listened very intently and at the end of the conversation accepted an earlier edition of this book to take with him.

In summary, a good question to have in our minds when we start witnessing to someone is, "Where is this person in relation to the Bible?" If he or she knows about the Scriptures and believes in them, then we would be wise to use them. If they are not conversant with them, then we'll need to be prepared to use the slower route that the apostle Paul took.

Secondly, it is also good to try and figure out whether or not they believe in the existence of God. Obviously the concept of the "blood of Jesus" is not going to mean anything to them if they don't believe that there is even a God. Many modern Buddhists in Bangkok, Thailand fit into this category. Therefore we need to gear our witnessing with this kind of person to the proving of God's existence, using of course, any common ground we can find.

A third question to consider is, "If they already believe in a Supreme Being, what is their image of God like? Does it need adjusting?" In many cases it does.

From here the next question to ask ourselves is, "Do they understand the concept of personal accountability?" Whereas some people consider God very harsh, others think He forgives and winks at just about anything. Those who have this way of thinking have to be graciously told otherwise. Are they now willing to repent?

Yet other questions to consider are, "Do they know who Jesus is? Does He have the place in their lives that is consistent with the fact that He is the only way to the Father, and that we are to live for him?" (2 Cor 5:5). That is, will they give their lives to Him?

The chapters that follow will expand on the truths that we need to present to those who are on different rungs of the "spiritual ladder." Our first consideration will be, "How do we speak to someone who doesn't believe in God's very existence?"

---

1. Taken from the NIV STUDY BIBLE, p. 1673. Copyright © 1985 by the Zondervan Corporation, Grand Rapids, MI. Used by permission.

Chapter Seven

PROVING GOD'S EXISTENCE

An atheist, a "free-thinker," and a pure Buddhist all have something in common. These people say they do not believe in the concept of God at all. How then, do we start witnessing to them? As we saw in the last chapter, the approach of the apostle Paul was to commence by talking about creation. In his letter to the church at Rome he was to later declare that God uses his handiwork to prove His existence (Rom 1:20). So let's start off with:

1) The Proof of creation.

Seated in the houses of common Thai people many years ago, I would ask the question, "Who made the world?" The usual reply was that they did not know. As I pointed out that one thing leads to another however, they seemed to catch on. They understood that a banana had to come from a banana tree, a baby came from its mother and a television set argues the existence of someone who put it together. They began to see that as everything else had a beginning and didn't "just happen," neither could creation "just happen" either.

In talking to the above-mentioned groups of people, I have sometimes pointed to the watch on my wrist and asked, "What kind of person would you think I would be if I were to tell you that this watch made itself? Suppose I were to tell you that over the process of time the sands formed the glass, that the metals came from the earth and formed the cogs, and that the other parts that form a watch also 'just came together?' Suppose I said to you that some nearby ox one day died so that its carcass formed itself into leather to produce the strap and that the buckle just appeared on the end?" They have taken my point that no one would accept such an explanation. I have helped them come to the conclusion that just as a watch with all its intricate parts cannot make itself, neither could creation around us produce itself either.

We need to continue from here to point out the superior creative attributes of this Creator. Not only does the watch in the above analogy argue the existence of a human designer, it also gives us an idea of what kind of designer was behind the making of the instrument. That is, he was obviously intelligent, careful, and someone who paid close attention to intricate details. Likewise, the world around us shows abundant evidence that this earth must have been created by someone whose intelligence far surpasses ours. Our bodies, for example, are a masterpiece of construction and engineering. Scientists tell us that the chemicals of our bodies are found in the ground. Now just suppose that we were able to shape the structure of a man. But even if we were talented in this realm, we would have no power to make the structure breathe, move and talk, let alone reason, digest food and produce children! There is Someone bigger, more powerful and more intelligent than you and me who put us together. It is in God that we live and move and have our being, and it's to Him we owe our love and allegiance.

Noel Gibson in his tract, *The Answer in Twenty Minutes* states that every part of our bodies is a masterpiece. We hear, he says, because of the vibrations of 24,000 "strings" in our ear mechanism. (A grand piano by comparison has only 240 strings and is a million times as big as one of our ears.) We see, Gibson continues, because of 137 million eye-seeing elements. Nor is it just the fact that we can see that is so marvelous. When our eyes are focused on near objects and then we look at far away ones, they refocus so fast we don't even notice it. Imagine if we had to readjust the focus of our eyes, as we do on a movie projector, every time we looked at a new object!

Our hearts pump approximately 40 million times a year for about 70 years without stopping for repairs. And what about the wonders of the lungs, the brain, the digestive system, the blood, the ligaments, the tissues and muscles of our extremely complicated make-up? Man's ability to reproduce himself is an amazing capability as well. Thinking scientists are awed by our genes. Physical characteristics, as well as traits of personality, are contained in something so small we can't even see it!

We can also mention the size of the universe in which we find ourselves. The distances within the universe are so mind-boggling that we have to use the term light-year to talk about distances in space. In order to describe a light year, perhaps the following reference to the U.S. space vessels would be useful. They fly at the astonishing speed of 25,000 miles per hour—that's about 44 times faster than the normal flight speed of a passenger jet today. A light year is the distance the space shuttles would have traveled in 27,500 years. When we consider the speed of light however, we are now talking of something faster again, because light only takes one year to cover what the shuttles would have taken 27,500 years to cover! At this lightning speed, light from the sun takes only eight minutes to cover the 91 million miles! But traveling at the same speed, it takes a lot longer to reach us from the nebula of Andromeda.

In fact, if that heavenly body were to self-destruct at this very moment, we would still be seeing light coming from it for the next 800,000 years! Or we can think of it another way. Suppose there was life on Andromeda. To send a radio message there from earth at the speed of light, it would take 800,000 years to arrive. We would then have to wait another 800,000 years for the reply! It gives the feeling of eternity, doesn't it?

But the galaxy of Andromeda just mentioned, is a very close galaxy to ours—so close in fact, that it is one of only three galaxies that can be seen from earth with the naked eye. Astronomers have photographed millions of galaxies through telescopes and believe there are *billions*.[1] Imagine the length of time that light (or radio messages) would take to reach the farthest galaxy which our radio-telescopes can see. Then think of the question that stares us in the face: "How far does the universe extend beyond the galaxies that our telescopes can pick out?"

But having just mentioned something of the *immensity* of the universe, let's consider for the moment the *density* of it. I can still remember as a twelve-year-old being amazed at the concentration of stars I saw as I looked through the telescope of an observatory. The part of the sky I was looking at was just a mass of fiery balls!

While the galaxy to which our sun belongs has a hundred billion stars, that is a relatively small amount of stars compared to some galaxies. To really get a picture of how many stars there are, we need to multiply the number of stars in a galaxy (100 billion in the "small" one we live in) with the number of galaxies we know of. I heard it once said that if all the stars in the universe had names and were printed in books, these books would cover an area the size of the State of Colorado (or the country of New Zealand) to a depth of ten feet! And that's just the stars of which we are aware. This points to the greatness of the Creator after whom we should seek.

Let's now consider the timetables that exist in the universe. We all know the moon circles the earth every 28 days. But while it is doing that, the earth itself (while the moon is circling around it) is revolving around our sun every 365 days. But that's not all. Other planets in our solar system also have moons that revolve around them. These planets in turn go around the sun taking varying lengths of time to do so. But then the whole solar system is also moving around the center of the Milky Way (the galaxy in which our sun is merely one lowly member among billions of others). It makes your head feel like spinning too, doesn't it?

Among all those heavenly bodies, just think of that which sets the earth apart. Our planet is about 91 million miles away from the sun. Scientists tell us that if we were 120 million miles away we would all freeze, whereas if it were only 60 million miles away we would all be burned. Then again, our sun is the right kind for us, for in the universe there are such things as super-suns. If one of these heavenly bodies were at the center of our solar system, its heat would turn the earth into a vapor.

Fortunately for us, the earth has a diameter that is smaller than that of the planets Jupiter or Saturn. Otherwise we humans would not be able to survive the tremendous pressure on our bodies of many tons per square inch. On the other hand, if the earth were smaller that it is, it would not be able to contain its moisture and the earth would not be able to sustain life. Neither would we have an atmosphere which filters out the harmful rays of the sun. Such an atmosphere for example, does not exist on the moon. That is why the astronauts who landed there years ago had to wear special suits to protect them from the deadly rays of the sun.

Could it happen then, that the size of the sun, the size of the earth, the distance of the earth from the sun, and even of the earth from the moon just happened by chance? No wonder the Psalmist in Psalm 19:1 exclaimed: "The heavens are declaring to their utmost the glory of God" (literal translation).

There are literally thousands of illustrations drawn from the amazing creation of the Supreme Architect that we can use in our witness to point to the existence of God. The fish that swim, the birds that fly, the insects that creep, the beasts that prowl, the lofty mountains, the flowing rivers and the immensity of the sea (and all that it contains) prove the existence of some great Being. Yet all the scientists in the world cannot make life, or a plant or even a blade of grass! And no wonder that the apostle Paul under the inspiration of the Holy Spirit wrote, "For since the creation of the world God's invisible qualities—his eternal power and divine nature—have been clearly seen, being understood from what has been made, so that men are without excuse" (Romans 1:20).

When proving the existence of God from creation, you need only use simple illustrations for country and tribal folk. For example, you could explain that if it were to rain all year there would be no crops, but if we were to live in continual sunshine we would be living in a desert. We can also talk about tasty food, how children can be so cute or some other fitting aspect about creation. Those people whose hearts are open will not require as much evidence as others will. Learn to collect illustrations as you hear of them, even tearing examples from newspapers or magazines. Let's remember the vision for world evangelism described in Chapter One!

Using creation to prove the existence of God is one extra-biblical route to employ. But there are also other things outside the Bible that point to the existence of God. Let's go on to:

2) The conscience.

In the opening pages of his book *Mere Christianity*, C. S. Lewis gives a powerful argument of how everyone is endowed with the sense of right and wrong. It's to this inbuilt sense of moral law for example, that a quarreling man appeals when he says, "That's not fair!" He's appealing to some kind of standard, Lewis says, which he expects the other man to know about.[2]

Our consciences therefore, confirm to us the existence of a moral ruler in this universe. If man has no one to whom he is responsible, why then, does he experience guilt over his misdeeds? Many will argue that conscience is just the result of environment and that statement is true to a large degree—environment does help shape our consciences. But at the same time conscience is more than that. For how is it that man can feel uncomfortable about his conduct, even when all around him are saying that what he is doing is perfectly all right?

When someone says, "There is no God. I have not heard Him speak," you could reply, "Yes He has. Can you remember that time you did something after a little voice said *don't do it*? Many times that is the voice of God!"

3) Personal testimony.

The use of our personal testimony is a powerful proof of the reality of God. The testimony of a changed life or the evidence of love in the environment of hatred or righteousness being lived out in a sinful society can all point to a higher power that motivates that righteous person—a power that transcends normal human behavior.

God's miracle-working power in the raising of cripples, the healing of the sick, the receiving of the sight for the blind gives adequate testimony to the existence of a Superior Being.

God's protection also speaks to people about His reality. More than one person could testify that in danger, some unseen, but not unfelt, force has physically moved them out of the immediate threat, and thus saved their lives. Our teenage son tells of the time when he was making a fort high up in a tree. One day with hammer in hand he slipped and suddenly there was nothing much between him and the ground. Yet he found himself miraculously "pushed" by Someone so that he could grasp a branch and save himself from bodily harm.

God's ability to provide also proves His reality. My wife and I have seen the hand of God's provision many times. Once, while based in Davao City in the south of the Philippines, Margaret and I felt impressed that I should travel to Munich, Germany. The occasion was the big YWAM evangelistic outreach that was about to take place during the 1972 Olympics. When I waved Margaret goodbye at the Davao Airport just before I flew off to Manila on a domestic flight, I had only $15 in my pocket and no ticket to Europe. I was trusting God for the provision for He had told me to go, but I had absolutely no idea where the money would come from. In Manila I waited. This wasn't the first time I had done something like this at God's prompting, but it was a test nonetheless.

Finally, while I was in Manila, Margaret informed me by a long-distance call from Davao that a letter had arrived in the mail from a perfect stranger in Australia—a man whom, to this day some sixteen years later, I have never met. He had no way of knowing of the compelling financial need I had at that time, yet the check he sent was for more than I needed to get to Munich. People glibly say there is no God. But when you trust Him for your bread and butter (and plane fares), He has just got to be there!

You may not have quite such a dramatic story to share. But I am sure you'll have your own stories to tell in many areas of your life as a result of your walk with the Lord which are just as *precious* to you. Don't be afraid to share these. There is power in giving testimony like this because it proves the reality of God. I'm told that a whopping 93 percent of communication is conveyed through the non-verbal. That is, through facial expressions, tone of voice and body language. Therefore, when you share the reality of God's involvement in your life, be it internal or external, provision or guidance, people will be able to sense that reality by your non-verbal communication and therefore more readily believe. As you share your personal experiences with the lost, try and be up to date. The more recent your stories are, the better. Actually, there are much more recent travel stories involving God's miraculous provision than the story of my going to Munich mentioned above (but they will have to be told in another book).

What we have been talking about in this chapter is that man knows Someone bigger than himself exists. It is a well known fact that hardened "atheists" have called on God when faced with death. This phenomenon has therefore given rise to the expression, "There are no atheists in fox-holes." It is interesting that anthropological research indicates that even in remote and primitive tribes there is a belief in "something" bigger than themselves. The sense of Someone greater is with all men and is strengthened by the things we see around us; the mountains and streams, the thunder and lightning, the sunrises and sunsets, the springtimes and harvest.

This sense that there must be Someone bigger than man is the reason why man must have a preoccupation with someone or something in his life. Unfortunately this devotion which should be directed to God is so often given to an idol, another created person or even an inanimate object like a sports car. Man is seeking self-fulfillment with something outside himself. The reason many teenagers are so bored today after "trying everything" is that they have not found what they were ultimately created for.

Proving the existence of God then, is our number one step in leading men from heathen or atheistic backgrounds to salvation. Now we must go one step further and consider God Himself.

---

1. "The World Book Encyclopedia" (Chicago, IL, Field Enterprises Educational Corporation, 1977), Vol 8, p. 8.
2. C.S. Lewis, "Mere Christianity," (New York, Macmillan Publishing Co., 1952) p. 17.

Chapter Eight

THE CHARACTER OF GOD

Although many believe in the existence of a Creator, not all have a good concept of His personal attributes. It is not just the Pagans or Hindus who fit into this grouping. There are many from Christian backgrounds who also need a greater picture of who God is too. Their image of Him is that of a harsh and unyielding despot—not someone with compassionate, father-like, forgiving characteristics.

In fact the term "God as a Father" is completely lost on many people. Their dads were strict, distant, or often absent. Their fathers didn't think up ways to have fun with their children, or they didn't convey to them that they were special. For many sadly, there was no father at all. For the children of these fathers then, the term "God as Father" doesn't communicate what it should.

This is very unfortunate because much of the image that we have of God is colored greatly by the opinion we have of earthly authorities over us—particularly the opinion we have of our dads. It is not only fathers who have contributed to this poor picture of God. Preachers who have been harsh have had their part in this too. Consequently for many, the concept of a loving God doesn't come easily.

Obviously with those with very little understanding of

Christian things, you are going to have to rely on the subject of creation again, through which God's "divine nature has been clearly seen" (Rom. 1:20). The apostle Paul also tells us that through creation we are all able to receive faith in Christ (Romans 10:17-18). That Scripture reads: " . . . faith comes from hearing the message . . ." But I ask: Did they not hear? Of course they did: 'Their voice [the voice of creation] has gone out into all the earth, their words to the ends of the world.' "

In other words, we can have faith in God's character, says Paul, because the things He has made tell us what He is like. Paul used common illustrations to prove this point by talking about food and gladness of heart as we saw in Acts 14:17. God could have made us capable of getting the fuel and energy we need for our bodies in a less appetizing way than He did. Suppose our food were to taste like foul-tasting medicine, for example, or sawdust or cement?

Now, think for a moment if He had made us with no elbows or knees. Can you imagine how difficult it would be to get into bed each night? Suppose we were not endowed with the powers of reason, imagination or memory? We would wake up in the morning and have forgotten all that we had ever learned—maybe even where we were or who we are! Think if God had created us without a voice and the powers of communication? Suppose we had no capacity to have friends and loved ones, no abilities to form friendships or use the emotions of joy, love or hope? If we are witnessing to those who are obviously parents, we can point out another act of God's goodness. They were given the privilege of being able to reproduce. As you use these illustrations and others that will come to you, people will start to realize that our God can be trusted because He is *good-natured.*

We may have heard the saying, "Power corrupts, and absolute power corrupts absolutely." In other words, selfishness does the greatest damage when it comes from a leader. The greater the leader the greater the damage if selfishness is employed. Some like Nero, Hitler and others have used their authority to maim, terrorize, torture and oppress their subjects. To accomplish their selfish ends, they have liquidated their opponents, sent millions to the gas chambers, or they have used their immense powers to stash millions of dollars into their personal accounts.

In contrast, even though God has more power than all earthly rulers put together, He is *good* and *loving* with His awesome abilities. His power is creative rather than destructive. Even when He tests us as Christians, it is for our good (Deut. 8:16).

"Why all this emphasis on the character of God?" you might ask. Because this is the heart of the gospel. We have to come to God for who He is—not for what we can get out of Him. The knowledge of who God is has to inspire us to do that. No other reason, I believe, really satisfies God for no other reason proves that the unsaved person is coming for unselfish reasons.

The analogy is drawn in Scripture between a man courting his bride and Christ wooing people to himself. It is a fitting analogy, principally because of the type of love that is required in both instances. A potential *husband* has to prove his unselfish love if he is going to win the heart of a young lady. Otherwise, how could she confidently expect his love and protection despite all difficulties? When we think of Christ's love for the Church, we, of course, have a similar parallel. There is no question that Christ unselfishly loves people. He is interested in them for their sakes.

In a similar fashion, unselfish love must characterize the *bride* in marriage too, otherwise that marriage will not last in the spirit that God intended. A young bride does not really love her bridegroom if the only reason she is marrying him is to leave an unhappy parental situation—a reason a lady once gave me for why she got married. In getting married, therefore, she was loving herself rather than unselfishly giving herself to her husband.

Neither would it be love if the only reason someone marries a man is because she was afraid of the knife at her ribs that he would jab into her if she refused. In the same way, being afraid of going to hell is not convincing proof of a love for God. It can even be unrefined selfishness. On the other hand, coming to God just to get to heaven is not a pure reason for approaching Him either. The only proof of our love is when we respond unselfishly to God just for who He is. That is, we are drawn to Him on the basis of His character. As we do this we come desiring to love and know Him *no matter what.*

This is one reason why God allows martyrdom. We all know He has the power to stop such seeming tragedies— but He doesn't always do that. He allows martyrdom on occasions to help us all purify our motives and to assess if we really are serving Him no matter what might happen. The killing of Christians down through church history has actually increased the numbers of those coming to Christ. For this reason, many of us may be called upon to give our lives for Him in order for the gospel to go to the ends of the earth. The unsaved are convinced that Christ must be real if they watch Christians lay down their lives for Him. Those who come to Christ during these periods of persecution, do so to please God—not to live happily ever after. Therefore they're strong Christians. These are the very people that God can use to further extend His kingdom.

It will be much easier to point out the character of God to those who are familiar with the Scriptures and the person of Jesus Christ. This is because Jesus was God and lived among us so we are even more able to understand what God was like through His life. We also see through Christ just how God wants us to operate in evangelism. The things that Jesus emphasized should therefore be the things that we emphasize. The aspects of the character of God that Jesus portrayed should be those which we exhibit. Let's look at just two of the times that Jesus was involved in personal evangelism. Firstly let's consider:

Christ's encounter with Zacchaeus.

One day, Jesus was passing through the hot Jordan Valley on His way to Jerusalem which lay 15 miles ahead in the Judean hills. He had no intention of stopping in Jericho as

He passed through (Luke 19:1). A large crowd, however, thronged the Jewish Rabbi whose miracles had given him national fame.

The region around Jericho was prosperous at the time and people were doing well. So too, were the tax-collectors who were collecting money for the Roman Government under the leadership of a despised man called Zacchaeus. Naturally, anyone doing the tax gathering was being a traitor to the Jewish nation and, as a result, they were a rejected group of people. Frequently, tax-collectors defrauded their own people as well, so they were doubly despised. Regarded as outcasts, they could not serve as witnesses or as judges and were expelled from the synagogue.[1] Zacchaeus was well known for his trade and was a rejected man as a result (Luke 19:7). After all, he wasn't just a tax-collector, he was a chief among them. And he was very rich (verse 2).

When Jesus came to town however, Zacchaeus wanted to see this renown Rabbi. But, as much as he tried, he was not able to because he was so short and the crowd so big. Whatever could he do? Driven by a compulsion to see this man whom many were calling the Messiah, he knew of only one way to do it. He would have to swallow his pride and climb a tree, even though he would look ridiculous perched up there in his robes. Running ahead of the slowly moving mass of people, Zacchaeus spied a sycamore tree along the path that Jesus was walking. Taking off his sandals, he gathered his flowing robes and scrambled up onto a branch that would support his weight. There, with breath panting as he recovered from his run, he waited.

Jesus came closer and closer until He was directly underneath. What a good view he was getting of Him! Then suddenly, Jesus looked up and started calling Him by name! Jesus' voice was so full of acceptance and compassion that Zacchaeus couldn't believe his ears.

What? Jesus wants to come to my house? He's not despising me? thought Zacchaeus.

Resolve suddenly filled Zacchaeus' heart in a way that

he had never felt before—determination to start a new life and give up defrauding people. People had made him feel so guilty and condemned that he could not get near enough to anyone in the local synagogue to even talk to them about spiritual matters. But this Prophet . . . He wants to come to my house?

Zacchaeus shinnied down the tree immediately. He could hear the crowd murmuring against Jesus for suggesting this idea of lunch in Zacchaeus' house. *All right then*, he thought, *I'll let them all know about my new resolve:* "Lord, right now I declare I will give half my possessions to the poor. I'm tired of just living for money. It's just not worth it. And if I have cheated anyone, I'll pay them back four times!"

Tears perhaps began to moisten Jesus' eyes. This was the kind of repentance He'd been preaching about for three years. He was delighted that He could see yet another person respond to His love and message before He went to the cross. And the four-fold restitution? *Well, it's four times what I require,* I can well imagine Jesus thinking, *but at least he won't be tempted to cheat again!*

"Zacchaeus, you're a saved man. You and your household are the very people I came looking for to bless and change."

Many moderns would have lost their opportunity in a situation like this by pointing bony fingers at him and by throwing him the demeaning line, "How can you escape the damnation of hell!" But God's character is not like that. Nor is the gospel. Otherwise it would not be good news. We capture something of the heart of God in Isaiah 57:16 which reads: "I will not accuse forever, nor will I always be angry, for then the spirit of man would grow faint before me . . . ." In Jonah 4:2, we get this description of the character of God: " . . . you are a gracious and compassionate God, slow to anger and abounding in love, a God who relents from sending calamity."

I love this about God. He looks for that lack in people, ministers to it, and then draws the individual away from his sin by overwhelming him with His love. What was

Zacchaeus' need at this point in time? I believe it was the need of being accepted—something that is recognized as being necessary by all human beings and something Zacchaeus wasn't receiving at the time he met Jesus. This need was met by Christ's *unconditional* love. That's the love that says, "I love you because of who you are, not because of how you have performed." It's the "I love you, not because of what you can do for me, but I love you in order to help you" kind of love. That is the love of *God.* And it ministers. It hits the mark. Instead of sending Zacchaeus away to cower and hide, it brought the best out of him. It brought him to "his knees" in his heart. Jesus, by his unqualified, unconditional, no-strings-attached love brought out the Zacchaeus that God had originally created, the noblest of all Zacchaeus. That is what God wants to do for everyone.

We, as the body of Christ, must learn that it is the character of God—His unconditional love—that motivates repentance. I have the feeling that the reason we have not evangelized the world is not because it cannot be done. It is not because we haven't done a lot of evangelizing either. Neither is it because we haven't spent a lot of money on it. Rather it is because we haven't shown *unconditional* love. The more of this kind of love the church shows, then the more "down-on-the-floor-thumping-the-rug" repentance we will see. The moral of this story is that the goodness of God leads us to repentance (Rom. 2:4).

Is the story of how Jesus treated Zacchaeus an isolated incident? The answer is no, for let's now consider:

Jesus' encounter with Simon Peter.

Think with me how you might feel if you had fought sleep off all night in order to earn a living. In Peter's case he had thrown out a fishing net and drawn it in empty all night and had caught absolutely nothing (Luke 5: 1-11). Think how disheartened he must have felt. Remember Simon Peter was a fisherman at this stage and not a disciple. He could very well have felt like swearing over the frustrating night he'd just experienced. It's possible that he might have been in great need for the fish to sell in order to buy basic food staples for that day. Galilee, in his day, was a poor and crowded place, like the Philippines is today. Many Filipino fishermen who catch nothing all night are not likely to eat the next day. Peter's situation may have been very similar.

He may not have been in a good mood that day. His felt need was to get out of the blues—not to feel that everything was going against him. He might even have felt that Jesus' sermon was totally redundant. Imagine his surprise when Jesus suddenly suggested that Peter go out fishing again, this time during the day. He protested, "Master, we've worked hard all night and haven't caught anything."

Yet he said he'd do it, probably because he had been impressed with the healing of his mother-in-law through a previous gracious act of Jesus (Luke 4:38-39). So, pushing his little fishing craft out into the blue waters again, he dropped his net over the side once more!

Then it happened. The biggest catch of fish Peter had ever seen. The net was at breaking point with the weight of the squirming fish! *This is what I need,* thought Peter. *More than what I need!* Immediately he contrasted his own sinfulness with the obvious loving care of a providing Heavenly Father who loved him! He was overwhelmed. *Things like this don't happen to sinful fishermen!*

"Depart from me, Lord," he bellowed. "I am a sinful man."

But Jesus didn't depart from him. Instead, our Lord promised him a fruitful spiritual ministry. As we draw this story to a close, we can see that Peter didn't just rise up, leave his nets and become one of our Lord's prominent disciples for no reason.

Peter sensed God loved him not just because of the physical fish—it was more than that. It was the sense that the Creator was interested in *him* and his frustrations. God proved again that He was *good-natured* just as he had proved this to Zacchaeus by ministering to the need of his aching heart.

xxx

Is this merciful approach of Jesus restricted then, to just these two incidents—His dealings with Zacchaeus and Peter? The answer is no, because you will remember that in Chapter One we saw Jesus use a similar approach when he dealt with the woman at the well. He honored her and lifted her sights to nobler levels. It is unfortunate therefore, that as we have witnessed, we have sometimes forgotten the heart of the gospel which Jesus defined as mercy.

We mentioned earlier that people should not come to Christ simply out of fear of going to hell. We must however, be true to the Word of God and believe in such a place. But there is no record through the pages of the New Testament of His mentioning hell in any of His one-on-one evangelism encounters. As He talked to the woman caught in adultery, to Mary Magdalene, Nicodemus and the Rich Young Ruler, He never used it as a "You've got to change or else" technique. Outstretched fingers pointed by square-mouthed preachers pronouncing hell, fire and brimstone was not Jesus' method when dealing with the man in the street. Stern words were reserved for the religious leaders of the day *who knew they were hypocrites.*

But this must not be construed to mean that we can talk tough to leaders of any religious group. Quite the contrary. Jesus was direct but not harsh when He talked to Nicodemus despite the fact he was a Pharisee. Jesus could see his heart—Nicodemus was seeking truth. This man's heart was so open that he later defended Jesus before the Sanhedrin (the Jewish internal parliament of the day) which was filled with our Lord's bitterest enemies. Later he spent good money on embalming Jesus' body (John 7:50, 19: 38-40). Jesus' forthrightness with the other Pharisees was that they were living in unrighteousness, yet were leaders of God's "church" of that day. They were not heathen priests. They knew what was right but didn't live in accordance with it. If Jesus were on earth today, His stern words would be reserved for any leader of His church who was living in unrighteousness and leading people astray. I think He would have strong words for a leader in the church who, say, was embezzling funds or who was cheating on his wife, and yet remained unrepentant. I believe he would have direct words to many Christians about the way they live during the week, yet come to the house of the Lord on Sunday. Jeremiah the prophet was sent by the Lord to the "professing Christians" of his day to deliver such a rebuking message. But I don't think Jesus would have us speak sternly to priests of non-Christian or pagan religions.

In his book, *Like a Mighty Wind*, Mel Tari tells the story of how a pagan priest in an animist area of Indonesia was giving a sacrifice to his "blood god." Suddenly Jesus came and revealed Himself to this pagan priest called Sam Faet who was suffering from leprosy.

"I am the God you are seeking." He said, "This is not the way to worship me."

"Lord, who are you and how do you want to be worshipped?" the priest asked.

"I will tell you my name and how to worship me later," Jesus said. "But first you must gather all your images and witchcraft materials and burn them. When you do this, I will visit you again and tell you all about myself." Then He disappeared.

Because Sam Faet was the high priest, the people obeyed his instruction and burned their gods. Then Jesus reappeared to the priest, and *healed* him of his leprosy. He also revealed who He was and gave instructions concerning salvation and the Christian walk. In turn, Sam Faet shared all this with his people who willingly accepted his message. When one of the teams from the Timor, Indonesian revival reached this village, they found a church in existence with Christians walking a holy life with Christ.[2] In the story just given, Jesus gently dealt with the pagan priest and healed him. This is again the application of the principle that the "goodness of God leads to repentance" (Rom. 2:4). In order to apply this principle we have to be very gentle and yet uphold God's truth at the same time. We also might be called upon to demonstrate much self-control and to extend forgiveness to people in order for them to see this principle being worked out in us before their very eyes! Let's be looking for ways to put this principle into practice!

****

In summary then, we can point to God's *creation* as a means of describing what He is like. We can also use Bible stories of Jesus' one-on-one contact with sinners as a portrayal of God's character. But perhaps the greatest way of all is by personally demonstrating God's character, either by personally *exhibiting Christ-like tendencies* in our own life or by miraculously *healing* someone like Sam Faet, who was healed of his leprosy. Or it could be by the personal demonstration of miraculous *provision* such as we saw in the story of Simon Peter. We should remember of course, that it's what it does to a person internally that will determine whether that person turns to God or not. If the person's *felt* need is met and they now feel "God is for me," they will be just that much more likely to respond to the Lord.

---

1. Taken from the NIV STUDY BIBLE, p. 1496.
   Copyright © 1985 by the Zondervan Corporation.
   Used by permission.
2. Mel Tari, "Like A Mighty Wind," (New Leaf Press, Green Forest, AR), p. 143-145. Used by permission.

Chapter Nine

MAN AND HIS SIN

When God created man in Eden, it was with the ability to love that which is good and to shun that which is evil. That capability is still evidenced by a mother cradling her baby to sleep, a son genuinely caring about the plight of his aged parents, or a young man respecting the needs of his bride-to-be. On the other hand, if man was to be created with freedom of choice, he had to have the capability (if he so desired) to love that which is evil and shun what is good. We certainly see abundant evidence of man's ability to do this. Our daily newspapers are full of stories of man's selfishness and brutality.

This ability to do either good or evil is couched in a wonderful liberty which we call the power of choice. Mankind would be a mere vegetable otherwise—living, but with no ability to determine his lifestyle or destiny. Naturally, as a result of all this, God took a risk when He entrusted us with this gift of choice. It was a calculated risk however, the same one we as parents take when we decide to start a family. We know that the children we bring into the world will have the potential to go astray and one day grow up to be prostitutes, gangsters or drunkards. Yet it doesn't usually stop us from having children. We trust that our offspring will not use their free wills to live immoral lives and we trust that they will love and honor us. So with

God. As much as He longed for our love and allegiance, He wasn't going to force it from us, for that wouldn't satisfy Him. With a heart bursting with love, He bestowed on us the beautiful creation that we have already described. He then waited expectantly for our loving response.

But the sad story of this world is that although we have had the ability to use our gifts and talents in a constructive way, we have used them selfishly. In the process, we have hurt not only the very God who gave us this free will, but those around us as well. No wonder God declared that He was "grieved that He had made man on the earth, and His heart was filled with *pain*" (Gen. 6:6).

The thing that hurt Him was what the Bible calls sin. What is sin? Let's consider some thoughts about it.

1) Sin is a choice.

Although we must be compassionate as we witness, we must not allow people to excuse their sin. The clear testimony of the Bible is that man is accountable for the wrong things that he does. Many will offer comments like "I cannot help myself," or "I am made this way." But, think for a moment. Do students cheat when the teacher is watching? Do thieves usually rob a bank in full view of armed security men on duty? Or do young people commit acts of sexual immorality in the presence of their parents? How is it then, that we can control ourselves on certain occasions, but at a midnight hour, when we think no one is watching, we suddenly cannot help ourselves?

If you are speaking to someone who is familiar with the Bible, you could direct their attention to the words of Jesus in Mark 7:21-23. Notice that Jesus lays the blame for our sin on our hearts—not on our neighbors or even our environment, although we know that these do influence us. But they are only *influences,* because they do not *cause* us to sin. Otherwise it would not be fair of God to punish us. This thought was promoted in the 1830's and was one of the contributing reasons why revivals broke out at that time. In fact, all the revivalists of the 1700's and 1800's, whether Armenian or Calvinist—Charles Wesley, George Whitfield, Charles Finney and others—stressed man's responsibility. That's why they saw the results they did.

2) Sin is being independent of God.

Simply put, the essence of sin is being independent of God. This, of course, can be expressed in a myriad of ways. It is finding significance and value in life without *depending* on Him. While some find meaning and comfort in life through drugs and crime, others worship at the altar of the arts—even respectable art, literature or music—leaving God completely out of their lives. Even as Christians we need to ask ourselves if our lives are being focused on God. David Wilkerson of *The Cross and the Switchblade* fame says he has learned to be suspicious of any activity in his life that he can't unhurriedly pray about.

3) Sin is an attitude — not just an action.

Many may feel that they have not sinned because they have not committed the "bigger" sins like murder, theft or adultery. Yet the inward sins may still exist nonetheless. Jesus taught that to hate was to "murder" and to have lust was to "commit adultery" (Matt 5:21-28). The other inward sins of pride, selfish ambition, jealousy and hate are just as deadly by the way—maybe even more so.

It is not only the obvious sins of commission like the cold shoulder, the bitter remark or the slashing of human flesh with a knife. It is also the sins of omission, like not helping to protect another's feelings, not helping with someone's burden of grief or not giving to those in obvious physical need when it is in our power and in the will of God to do so.

Some people may say that they have done nothing wrong. We must point out that even the best person in the world has not always followed God to his utmost. Most people will agree that they have left God out of their lives on many occasions and have not been completely iden-

tified with His purpose. They will also agree that they have
passively looked on evil and have not been interested in
endeavoring to wholeheartedly make this world a better
place.

4) Our sin affects others.

Some, of course, are genuinely bothered about the state of
the world and ask "Why do the innocent suffer?" We could
think of it this way. If I were to get into a car and disobey
the rules of the road and kill some innocent pedestrian, it
would not be the car manufacturer's fault nor the fault of
the government that made the rules of the road. It would
be *my* fault. My sin would have caused the innocent to
suffer. Likewise in this world, if we do not obey God,
others will be affected negatively. If I lie, steal and get
angry in an unrighteous manner, others will get hurt.
Innocent people suffer in wars because man's sin affects
others. It is certainly not God's fault, for He has told us
many times what to do through the voice of our
consciences.

5) The knowledge that sin is wrong is universal.

All men know the difference between right and wrong.
Man knows he ought to do differently than what he does.
This sense of "oughtness" is revealed when man judges
others. In a sense it will be man who will be able to judge
himself on Judgment Day. Possibly on that day we will be
able to see videos of ourselves on which we'll hear all the
times we've told others what to do and what not to do. But
at the same time we'll be able to see ourselves (by way of
another video) doing the very opposite! In this way we'll be
passing judgment on ourselves! The Bible warns us that
every mouth will be silenced and the whole world will be
held accountable to God (Rom. 3:19).

   "When did this sense of 'oughtness' enter the world?"

you might well ask. That took place in the Garden of Eden. Adam and Eve had those instructions written *on their hearts* and so has every person who has entered the world since then. Several generations before the Ten Commandments came on tablets of stone, the wife of Potiphar repeatedly asked a young Israeli called Joseph to lie with her. He refused each time, despite the fact that he was far from home. Finally he exclaimed, "How ... could I do such a wicked thing and sin against God?" (Gen. 39:9). Joseph did not have to wait for a prophet called Moses to inform him, "You shall not commit adultery." This law is written on every man's heart. Therefore, it shouldn't be that hard for us to lovingly point out that one day God will hold all men accountable for his sins.

****

It is necessary to take time to explain this subject of sin carefully. Many people simply quote Romans 3:23, "for all have sinned and fall short of the glory of God" and feel that the mere quoting of this Scripture is adequate in itself. Actually in its context this verse makes an interesting study. Paul started his discourse about the sinfulness of man in the first chapter of the book of Romans. In order to prove his point he uses many examples, among them the list in Romans 1:29-30. Included are the sins of greed, malice, ill will, cruelty, the sins of the mouth, hatred and all forms of pride.

In Romans 3:23 then, after almost three chapters of building his case and explaining of sin in *experiential terms,* only then does he come to the climax of his argument and say, "for all have sinned and fall short of the glory of God." We would do well to follow Paul's pattern and explain what sin really is.

Yet, although we as men and women are to blame for the suffering in this world, God doesn't give us the cold shoulder and walk away. He weeps with us, knowing our hurt. Why? Because He lovingly wants to alleviate the load we are carrying and remove the burden of our guilt. What a God! We must always plan therefore, to represent this God fairly as we talk about sin, which we must do. And we must try to represent His heart as we talk about this necessary subject. If we do have to use the word hell, we would represent God better if we do it with tears in our eyes. In this way we'd be exhibiting His character. We'd be conveying to the sinner that we don't want him to go there and God doesn't want that either. He'll more easily respond to that kind of approach.

For people to be saved there has to be an acknowledgment of sin, and that is not always easy for everyone to do. But we as Christian workers can greatly help in this area. An accepting, loving Christian (the kind of person who knows what it is to have his eyes mist up as he listens to someone's confession, is the person who will help a sinner tremendously). People will tell us everything if they know they will still be loved and accepted by us after they have finished. In fact, I don't believe we have the right to expect others to break down under the conviction of sin in our presence unless they do sense we love them. And the poorer the self-image the sinner has, the softer the soulwinner's heart must be. The reason for that is actually quite simple. A certain level of self-image is necessary in order to break one's heart open before the Lord. One of the ways to build up a person's self-esteem (so they can do that breaking) is for him to feel loved by our unconditional acceptance. I believe this explains why Jesus spoke this way to the woman at the well (John 4), to Zacchaeus (Luke 19), and to Simon Peter (Luke 5). He was, of course, much more direct with the Rich Young Ruler (Mark 10) and Nicodemus (John 3). Maybe the self-esteem of the last two named was far more intact.

However, no one can say at the judgment, "I'm going to hell because no one loved and accepted me." They can't say that because the whole of creation cries out that there is a loving God in the universe. Later we'll see that the cross of Christ joins in this message to say the same thing. Yet, there is no getting away from the following fact: We as soft, tender-hearted counselors can be the very catalyst that will swing the balance of power in the struggle that rages in a sinner's heart—especially when he wonders whether he'll trust God, or go his own selfish way.

****

I have found that if I mention to people certain of the sins that I have formerly been involved in, this helps them to acknowledge their sin. But there is an art in this. We have to exhibit the solemnity that befits the fact that we have hurt God and wounded others. At the same time there has to be that softness in our heart that will prompt them to believe they can tell us that they lied, stole, got angry or "slept around." As a general rule, boys should not share about their former sexual misdeeds to a girl in a witnessing situation and vice versa. In most non-Western countries however, you probably shouldn't be witnessing one-on-one with a member of the opposite sex anyway.

It is also good to gently mention the sins that weren't your downfall as well, so that the Holy Spirit can softly touch their hearts. After all, it is the Holy Spirit, Jesus said, who would convict the world of sin (John 16:8). We were all born with consciences. But through constant misuse the conscience of the person to whom you are witnessing may not be functioning very well. However, the Holy Spirit can take your words spoken in love and start the process by which they become aware that certain things are indeed wrong. Anger is always a good illustration to use, because at some time or other most have lost their temper. You might like to ask in a kind way, "Do you get angry sometimes?" Explain to people that there is a small voice inside us that tells us not to do things, but we deliberately and willfully go ahead and do them anyway.

Having read all the foregoing, you will agree that we are not called to the ministry of condemnation. You'll also agree, I hope, that we can never rejoice about hearing another Christian, fresh from a witnessing situation say, "I really gave it to them."

There is one last point I would like to make before

this chapter closes, and it is this: When we travel abroad from a Western country to a non-Western country, the need for a soft heart is intensified, in some instances, a hundred-fold. Like it or not, if we are white-skinned, we represent (to some minds) the colonial powers that formerly ruled that country—a Western country that may have governed in an unjust way. It is common knowledge that Great Britain forced China last century to open its doors to trade. Opium was deliberately introduced so that thousands of Chinese people became addicted in order to enhance Britain's chances to trade with that nation.

In other countries, such as in Asia, Africa, the Pacific, and Latin America, many injustices were perpetrated by the colonial powers. The hurts of those wounds have sometimes been passed on from generation to generation. For us to preach condemnation upon non-Westerners with vigor and insensitivity will diminish our ability to be a tool in the hands of the Holy Spirit. Remember too, that the West does not have a great track record to boast about in other areas of life either. The West has a high incidence of AIDS, a high divorce rate (even among Christians), and is responsible for so much moral pollution that is exported via the medium of motion pictures, magazines and tourism. America, Europe, Canada, Japan, Australia, New Zealand and South Africa all have levels of moral decadence. It behooves us therefore, to preach and mention sin with a very soft heart—the kind of heart that God would want us to have.

Chapter Ten

A QUESTION TO BE ASKED

During the last few chapters we have discussed three important truths: The existence of God, the character of God and the knowledge of right and wrong that mankind possesses. These are three important concepts, by which every man and woman will be held accountable before God. It will be just as true for the man without the Bible as the man with it. Drug addicts, murderers, gamblers, drunkards, adulterers and even those living in the deepest jungles will be held accountable to God on this basis. *Everybody is aware of these three truths.*

This should be a great encouragement to us, for it means that as we witness to those without a Christian background, we can have confidence that we are reaffirming things that they know deep inside, whether they admit it or not.

These truths may be distorted, for sure, but they will be there nonetheless. Or they were there at one time, for the Bible does teach that a conscience can be hardened by willful wrong action (1 Tim 4:2). Nobody however, is born that way. Man can get to a stage where he can commit crimes without any bad feelings, but God still holds him responsible for the deliberate deeds of disobedience that have blunted the working order of this God-given internal monitor of right and wrong.

But no one however, is beyond hope if he wants help. Nicky Cruz of *The Cross and the Switchblade* story is a case in point. By carefully going over the things mentioned in the previous three chapters with someone, I feel a good conscience can be restored, especially if the person starts choosing to live in the light of what he knows to be right, regardless of what his emotions may say.

The understanding of these three concepts also gives God a righteous basis for judgment, regardless of whether a man has heard of Jesus or not. If a tribal man starts living up to the light of the knowledge he has received (which includes at least the three concepts we have been discussing), and begins seeking the Lord, he will be rewarded by further revelation. Stories are told similar to the one we shared earlier about Sam Faet in Timor. Pagans in dark areas of the world have cried out to God and have been given revelation which has eventually resulted in understanding about the cross of Christ; for only in Jesus is there salvation (Acts 4:12). Their seeking God has also led to their eventual conversion, just as Sam Faet came to know Christ.

Man therefore, is accountable. But many times we spoil our testifying because we offer the *remedy* without first giving any understanding of man's terrible *malady*. We need to bring our listeners to the point where they realize that they have not been living in a way consistent with the overwhelming evidence for the love of God. Instead, they have been living for themselves. In a kind way, we must now face our friends with their accountability by asking the question: "How can someone approach a holy and good God and live in harmony with Him when they have sinned so deliberately against Him?" At this point, pause in the conversation. Let the Spirit of God speak, and let them think.

While they are doing this, they could easily be coming to the realization that something has to be done. To have told them the remedy at the beginning of the conversation, can spoil the Holy Spirit's work of conviction of sin (John 16:8). Remember, without conviction there can be no repentance and without repentance there can be no salvation (2 Cor 7:9-10).

On many occasions, when a conversation has lapsed into small talk, I have found that this question has brought the listener back face to face with his problem and the need to find a solution.

As an answer to our question, some will say that if they pray, God will forgive them. However, we must make it clear to them that this is inadequate in itself. Suppose a man murdered someone, was tried, found guilty and sentenced to be executed. What good would it do if that man were to fall down before the judge and pray, "Please forgive me!"? This is a question I have often asked my listeners and usually the answer is, "The judge cannot just forgive him and let him go. The murderer must be punished." This is the answer we need, for our listener will now understand that God cannot forgive us as simply as that. Even our governments could not maintain law and order if a man could be so easily forgiven. People would not be secure because of the rise there would be in murders, robberies, assaults and so on. We need to tell people that God cannot forgive us merely on the basis of prayer alone. Something has to happen to us *internally* before God could be just and yet justify us as deliberate sinners. Allow this truth to sink in. Do not rush in and explain the basis on which they can be forgiven just yet.

Many people fail to see that God would have been just to condemn the world and punish us all for our sin. He did not have to send an answer and it is good for people to realize this. But He did, and the solution He arrived at allows us to see a more full expression of His character—both as to His love and His righteousness. We will see this now as we move on to our next step . . . .

Chapter Eleven

JESUS CHRIST AND THE ATONEMENT

Now it is time for us to introduce the concept that although we are accountable for our sin, someone came to earth to provide the opportunity for the forgiveness of that sin. But this was someone more than a mere human being. It had to be someone who was both sinless and divine, and so this necessitated the coming from heaven of a Divine Person. Now the idea of God coming to earth was not completely foreign to the thoughts of ancient men. Several centuries B.C., the philosopher, Socrates, said if God wished to influence this world it would be necessary for Him to become a man. The Jews, of course, had the expectation of a Heavenly Deliverer or Messiah. But God had planned from the foundations of the earth to send such a Person to release us from both the penalty and practice of sin.

But what evidence is there that Jesus Christ really is God's Son and equal to God the Father? At one point He said, "I and the Father are one" (John 10:30). That's a big claim. Was He lying or telling the truth? Was He deceived, even lunatical? Or can the person of Jesus Christ be best explained away as merely a legend—someone who really didn't exist at all? Let's look at all these possibilities by starting with the thought that:

1) He was a legend.

The Bible states there was such a person as Jesus Christ and records His birth, life, teachings, death and resurrection. Other documents from antiquity do as well. We know, for example, that He was counted in a Roman census. Josephus, a very famous Jewish historian mentions Him as do Pliny the Younger, Tacitus and Suetonius.[1] That hardly qualifies Him to be a legend. Let's look at another possibility.

2) He was a lunatic.

Many people are prepared to accept Jesus as a great teacher but say they cannot accept His claims to Deity. They are saying by that statement that Christ was deceived. How can they then, put such confidence in the teachings of a person who says he is the Almighty when he is not? You can't, because if he were deceived on something like that, think of all the other things he could be wrong about.

But consider for a moment the kinds of things He said. Like, " . . . do to others what you would have them do to you" (Matt. 7:12). No wonder those who were sent to arrest Him came back empty-handed saying, "No one ever spoke the way this man does" (John 7:45-46). And then think of the way that Jesus was concerned about His mother when He was on the cross. He spoke to the apostle John to take care of her after His death (John 19:25-27). A lunatic would not be that unselfish and caring. The description of Jesus being a lunatic doesn't sit well either. Let's then consider the third alternative.

3) He was a liar.

Jesus' unique claim to being God was not tied to his miraculous powers alone. Human beings (especially biblical characters) have wrought similar miracles to those Jesus performed, both before and after His time on earth.

But central to His claim to Deity is His declaration that He would rise the third day after He was crucified. If He didn't rise from the dead, then He was a liar.

A British journalist saw this very point many years ago and thus set out to do research and prove for all that Jesus Christ most certainly did not rise from the dead. The result of His study was the book, *Who Moved The Stone*, in which he traces the paths that he took in his search to disprove the resurrection. But his research led him to be confronted with the evidence that Jesus did indeed rise from the dead.[2] One powerful evidence for the resurrection is the empty tomb and the missing body. Some have said that the disciples must have stolen it. That would be hard to believe for they didn't have much chance with the Roman soldiers guarding the tomb. But suppose in their zeal (which they certainly didn't have at the time of Christ's crucifixion), they found weapons and overthrew the soldiers—would they have gone through all the persecution they endured for what they knew was a hoax? Would James have let himself be killed by the sword for preaching the resurrection when he knew where the body of Jesus was? That doesn't make sense.

"Well, then," some have said, "the Jews must have stolen it." But that's hardly logical either, because the Jews would have trotted out the body of Jesus for all to see. It would thus put the apostles to shame and have closed the case once and for all. Nobody would have believed the apostles or have become followers after that. And the Romans? They would have loved to have had the body too, as it would have rid them of the "sect of the Nazarene," which in their mind was fermenting trouble in their world. There is therefore one other alternative:

4) He was telling the truth.

The greatest proof that Jesus is indeed God is His triumphant resurrection from the dead, which is recorded in the Bible, and proved by historical evidence. Josephus, the ancient historian wrote this concerning Christ around the year 93 A.D: "Now there was about this time, Jesus, a wise man, if it be lawful to call him a man, for he was a doer of wonderful works—a teacher of such men as receive the truth with pleasure. He drew over to him both many of the Jews and many of the gentiles. He was [the] Christ, and when Pilate, at the suggestion of the principle men among us, had condemned him to the cross, those that loved him at first did not forsake him, for he appeared to them *alive* again the third day as the divine prophets had foretold these and ten thousand other things concerning him; and the tribe of Christians, so named from him, are not extinct at this day"[3] (Emphasis added).

God's miracle power helps us demonstrate the reality of the resurrection and therefore, the Deity of Christ just as it did in Bible days. This is evidenced by the healing of the sick and the transformation from lives of vice and immorality as a result of people following Jesus as their Lord. We should also be aware that the Holy Spirit, who is in the world to convince men about the truth of Christ's claims, will endorse the words we say as we declare the truth of Christ's Deity. If we are dealing with those who are familiar with the Bible, we can point to the Scriptures that prove that Jesus Christ is God. Here are some of them: In Romans 1:4 we read, "[He] was declared with power to be the Son of God by his resurrection from the dead: Jesus Christ our Lord." In referring to the blood that Jesus shed (Acts 20:28), Paul calls it the blood of God, thus equating Jesus Christ with the Almighty.

Paul is not the only New Testament writer that has this belief. The apostle John opened his gospel with the statement, "the Word was God" (John 1:1). Further in that chapter we read that the apostle is referring to Jesus Christ when he refers to "the Word" (1:14). The same apostle refers to the term "Word" in the book of Revelation which he also wrote. There the term is equated with the King of kings and Lord of lords (Rev. 19:13,16).

The writer of the book of Hebrews tells us that the angels of God are to worship Christ, yet we are told throughout the Bible that no other than God is to be worshipped (Deut.6:13, Matt.4:10, Rev. 19:10). Hebrews 1:3, together with Colossians 1:15 and 2:9, reveal that Jesus Christ is the image of God and identical to Him. We will let Hebrews 1:8 have the last say here: "But about the Son he says, Your throne, O God, will last for ever and ever . . . . "

****

Although Jesus was God and came from heaven, this does not automatically put the world right with the Godhead. It wasn't that the Trinity found it difficult in their heart to forgive us. I trust there has been enough said in the foregoing chapters to see how loving and how prepared to forgive God has always been. Actually it could be said that God has an obsession to justly forgive us. The problem that God had, we might say, was the need to uphold His justice and preserve law and order while extending His forgiveness. Many perhaps, do not appreciate the dilemma He had, but maybe the following story will serve to make this clearer.

There was once a king called Zeleukas who made a rule that if anybody was found guilty of committing adultery they would have both their eyes plucked out. The rule was announced and became law, with King Zeleukas having every intention of enforcing it. Then one day the unthinkable happened. A young man broke that law, was arrested and summarily brought before Zeleukas. Imagine the pain in the king's soul, however, when he recognized that it was his own son who stood before him! His heart went out to his own flesh and blood whom he naturally wanted to forgive. Immediately he was in a dilemma. If he spared him, then justice would not be upheld. But on the other hand, how was he going to bring himself to issue the command to have the eyes of his son gouged out?

After some painful deliberation he came to his decision. In order to uphold public justice and preserve law and order, he could not back down and waive his law just to accommodate his son. People would neither respect him nor the law-enforcement process if he did. Accordingly, the day for the removal of the son's two eyes arrived. Both the kingly law-giver and his guilty son presented themselves during the eye-removing procedure. It was a gruesome sight as they began to gouge out the son's first eye. The young man let out a piercing scream while the king's soldiers held him firm. The king then motioned for the man in charge of the ceremony to now gouge out the second eye. But instead of directing their attention to the second eye of the boy, the king beckoned his soldiers towards himself. He then pointed to one of his *own* eyes. Those watching from the gallery gasped! The soldiers proceeded with the ceremony and stabbed a short sword into the king's right eye removing it completely. Grimacing in agony and holding both hands over the now empty eye socket area, the king's servants lead him away into privacy.

The event that those in the gallery had just witnessed quickly became the talk of the town. But the logic of the king's move became very clear over the ensuing days. He had extended partial forgiveness, at great cost to himself. But at the same time he lay another foundation to last for a long time to come. That foundation was people's respect for both the law-giver and the law itself.

The problem that King Zeleukas faced was very similar to the problem God had to solve. Although He loved man and was committed to doing the best possible for him, He still had to uphold his justice and righteousness which is also built on love. Sin, God knew, could never be encouraged because that brings forth unhappiness, unfulfillment and ultimately spiritual death. Whatever could He do?

His answer was the shedding of blood, and He conditioned men to this right from the moment Adam and Eve revolted against His rule in Eden. Imagine with me the trauma our first parents must have gone through watching blood being shed from the very animals they had loved and named. The killing of these animals was necessary to provide the garments made of skins that God gave them in exchange for the fig leaves that they had made (Gen. 3:

21). Think how they must have sobbed over the loss of these precious innocent animals. They may have resolved never to disobey God again.

Many fail to see God's tender overtures to woo Adam and Eve back to Himself in this garden story—even though they lost the privilege of staying in Eden. God's first desire is never punishment for punishment's sake. He is never vindictive. That concept is vividly illustrated through what we have discussed about the life of Jesus as a one-on-one evangelist. God's first reaction to sin is that of redemptive love. Redeeming a man to his original purpose is always God's first priority. God continued to condition men over the centuries through the shedding of the blood of animals. Without the shedding of blood there is no forgiveness (Heb. 9:22). It was done with the purpose of deeply humbling the proud heart of mankind into loving submission by encouraging an *internal* work to be done in the heart of man—not just a legal standing.

Think with me about the effect that the annual Day of Atonement had upon the lives of a little Jewish boy and girl in a typical Jewish home. Three weeks before the great day, father would bring home a little lamb for the coming sacrifice. The children would fall in love with the animal and would play with it at every opportunity. Then the sacrificial day came and they would weep as they learned that the lamb was going to be offered. They would be heartbroken with just the thought of the local Jewish priest plunging the knife into the throat of their woolly friend. But if they watched the blood spurt as the little lamb struggled and then became limp, we can all imagine how they must have felt. A good father would have used the occasion to gently teach his offspring about how awful sin was to God. And there must have been deep impressions made each Day of Atonement upon their little hearts that would not be easily erased. *My sin must be horrible to necessitate the death of my pet.*

We have seen that the blood of these animals was not the *only* condition to be met for the offerer to be cleansed of his sin. It was also necessary that the worshipper respond with repentance to the shedding of the blood. If the sacrifice produced the necessary brokenness of heart and persuaded the offerer not to sin, then God's purposes were fulfilled (Micah 6: 6-8). That portion of Scripture reads, "With what shall I come before the Lord . . . shall I come before him with . . . offerings, with calves a year old? Will the Lord be pleased with thousands of rams . . . ?" The prophet then explains what pleases the Lord. They are the things which were to be produced in the *heart* of the offerer through the shedding of the blood. They involved acting justly, loving mercy and walking humbly with our God.

The psalmist conveyed the same thought when he declared, "You do not delight in sacrifice . . . in burnt offerings. The sacrifices of God are a broken spirit; a broken and a contrite heart . . . " (Ps. 51:16-17). Through the shedding of blood, God was *just* by discouraging sin and at the same time *merciful* by freely forgiving.

So we can understand why God instituted the practice of having animals slain for sin in the Old Testament. He wanted to graphically illustrate that sin is horrible. Alas, modern man has all but lost this concept. We won't have revival until this principle is recaptured—not by legalistic ways but by being overwhelmed by the understanding of both the love and holiness of God.

****

Now, the normal Jewish mode of execution in the days of Christ, you will remember, was by stoning. Several carefully aimed rocks could have easily killed Jesus Christ. But God chose the awful cross. Why? The reason is this. God chose the cross to affect brokenness of heart from people in an even greater way than was accomplished through the offering of animal sacrifices. He deliberately made it horrible to break the heart of man over sin and to deter him from it.

When a friend of ours in the Philippines watched the crucifixion scene in Franco Zeffirelli's movie, *Jesus of*

Nazareth, she mentioned that people were crying all over the theater. I heard of one Buddhist lady in Malaysia who also cried watching this movie and subsequently came to the Lord. This is *exactly* the effect that God intended to happen through the cross. Thus humbled at the cross over sin, cleansed by His blood and convinced of God's unfathomable love, man can rise in gratitude and praise to humbly serve his King (1 John 1:7).

In the earlier story about king Zeleukas, we can imagine the moral power that the king's suffering had upon his son. It would not be hard for us to believe that the son could have been extremely humbled over his father's sacrifice. In love for his father, and in gratitude to him for still having part of his eyesight, I can imagine the boy resolving to never be immoral or disobey his father again.

But imagine with me the justice the king upheld and the moral force that would have extended throughout his kingdom. Whenever his subjects saw the king walking around with only one seeing eye, it was a pointed reminder that the king had unswerving moral standards. In the same way, the cross shows that God does not treat sin lightly and that His moral standards are to be maintained. Through the cross, God is *just* in that He rightfully discourages sin, but at the same time He extends the opportunity for *mercy.*

We see too, that the biblical sacrifices are quite different from the sacrifices performed by pagans. For in heathen sacrifices, sin is seen as dealt with in a way which allows the offerer to continue in his sin, just because a sacrifice has been offered. Jesus' death is a *provision* for our sin, but we are not free to continue in sin, just because Jesus died. Humbled and broken by his *substitutionary* death, we rise from our knees completely changed to live in righteousness and communion with God.

As noble as King Zeleukas' sacrifice was for his son, it does not really compare with what Jesus did for us. For one thing, Jesus gave his whole life in sacrifice for us, not just one eye. Nor do we have just partial vision. He has redeemed us completely. May we humbly praise Him for that day after day. We should never lose the thrill that this

Creator God, with all His imagination, ingenuity, and skillful powers should condescend to become a mere man and make provision for our forgiveness.

This then, is the solution to man's problem of sin. A loving God made man in His own image to live righteously, but man willfully lived for himself and those things that gave him meaning without God. Being the Person that He is, God still wanted to go out of His way to help man and restore him to his earlier happiness. He gave us this chance by sending His Son to be the substitution for the punishment for His creatures' sin.

God would have been extremely just to have punished the world, wipe it clean of sinners, and start afresh. The fact that He sent Jesus Christ to save man from his sin is a greater revelation of His character. It upholds the principle of justice because sin is discouraged, but it also demonstrates God's obsession with finding a way to be merciful. That, my friend, is the God we must present to the public. Let's do it!

****

If you have been following the suggested witnessing pattern of this book, you have now shown your friend much of the pathway back to God. Many Christians would, at this stage, ask for a committal to Christ using the oft-repeated phrase, "Do you want to accept Jesus?" But I would not suggest this because it is so easy for the listener just to say "yes" to please us, especially in the non-Western world. Remember what we mentioned in the *Before We Begin*...section. Hindus, for example, believe that truth is not the real facts, but rather what they perceive their listeners want to hear. It is not just Hindus who act like this either. Consequently, whenever you ask a question, phrase it in such a way that a "yes" or "no" answer is impossible. Ask questions that require a thoughtful answer of at least one sentence. A good way to do this is to start any question with the words "what?," "where?," "why?," "who?," and "how?"

Instead of asking, "Do you want to receive Jesus?," you might want to put the question this way: "You have heard what we have said about God, sinful men and the Lord Jesus Christ. What do you think your response should be to all this?" If the listener does not offer an answer, then obviously he or she is not ready for salvation. If they were, surely they would say something. Wouldn't a man who knew his house was on fire, call for someone to put it out? Shouldn't men who have sinned against the loving heart of God say something like, "I want to get right with the Lord and be forgiven by Him!"?

If the listener does indicate that he wants Christ and forgiveness, it is probably wise to delay him from praying just yet. There are important things that would be best for him to understand. We will discuss these in the next chapter. So far we have talked about God's initiative in salvation. Now we must deal with what God requires of man . . . .

---

1. Floyd McClung, "Dead Men Don't Think," pp. 3,5.

2. Frank Morison, "Who Rolled The Stone," (Downer's Grove, Ill., InterVarsity Press.

3. "Josephus, Antiquities of the Jews," (Grand Rapids, Michigan, Kregel Publications, 1960), Book XVIII, Chapt. 3; Section 3.

Chapter Twelve

REPENTANCE

The fact that Jesus Christ came to earth does not automatically solve the problem of man's sin. God's sacrifice of His Son still requires man's response before it can become effective in the lives of individuals. From the annals of the history of the United States comes an amazing story which illustrates what I mean.

George MacKintosh (not his real name) had been condemned to death by a U.S. court for committing a violent crime. He now sat in his cell on death row where the days passed slowly as he awaited the day of his execution. But George had a friend on the outside who cared for him—a friend who had considerable influence with the State Governor from whom he was able to procure a pardon. I can just imagine how excited the friend might have been as he took the Governor's signature to the prison—anticipating the delight on George's face! But, for some strange reason that we do not understand, George refused to accept it.

This left the authorities in a dilemma. What happens if there is provision for a man's release and pardon, but he refuses to walk out of jail? A special court case had to be called to decide the fate of the prisoner. After careful deliberations, the decision handed down was: "The pardon was valid only if the condemned man would receive it. Because he has rejected it, the pardon cannot take effect."

After the execution, no one was sadder than the friend who had worked for George's release.

The parallel of that story to mankind today is striking. Although Jesus' death was the provision for everyone's salvation, forgiveness cannot take effect until there is a submission to His loving lordship. These are His terms. When people refuse His loving overtures and miss out on His pardon, no one is sadder than He.

We shall endeavor to go very carefully into the subject of what we must do, because it is at this point, I believe, that many of our mistakes are made in witnessing. We have a tendency to rush in and pray the sinner's prayer with someone before he or she is ready. Just as danger can be caused to a baby through a premature delivery, so too can damage occur in the life of an individual who is led in a sinner's prayer before the proper time.

If you have been following the witnessing pattern suggested in this book, perhaps now you are coming close to leading that person to Christ. It would be an advantage if the person being witnessed to is convinced at this point of the authority of the Word of God. (Reasons why we can have faith in the Word of God are given in the appendix of this book.) We are now going to rely heavily on the Bible as our authority. This is done so that you may receive a better understanding of what must occur before someone is ready to enter God's kingdom. The following is explained in detail, although usually only the gist of what is said here need be shared with an inquirer.

Our first consideration has to do with the word *repentance,* which means forsaking things we know are wrong. Repentance has to be understood as being different from confession. A person can admit that he broke into someone's house, for example, but unless he stops such activity, his confession has not led to repentance. Confession is admitting that we have sinned. Repentance is the forsaking of that sin.

What then, are we required to turn from? There are six things:

1) We are required to turn from sin.

We have already defined sin as selfishness. We have also seen that we sin when we receive our sense of significance and purpose in life from things instead of from the Lord. Sin is saying we know better than God by the life-style we pursue. It is also rebellion against His loving rule and right over our lives. However, I believe it would be helpful for us to look at the fruits of this rebellious heart against God. Three times the apostle Paul is led by the Spirit of God to list sins, which, if committed and not repented of, will exclude us from God's kingdom. These lists are found in Galatians 5:19-21, Ephesians 5:5 and 1 Corinthians 6:9-10. The apostle John records a supplementary list in Revelation 21:8. To familiarize ourselves with these passages of Scripture would be an asset to our understanding of what God considers sin. Note that the worshipping of idols and sexual sins are mentioned in each list, while stealing, lying, witchcraft, murder, hatred, jealousy, slandering and wild parties also are mentioned. These things speak of rebellion against laws. We actually see much of the Ten Commandments in these three lists. To repent then, is to make a deliberate, conscious act to leave behind the things mentioned above, by the grace of God.

2) We are required to turn from the world.

The apostle John writes in his epistle, "Do not love the world or anything in the world. If anyone loves the world, the love of the father is not in him" (1 John 2:15). The book of James records a similar passage, " . . . don't you know that friendship with the world is hatred towards God. Anyone who chooses to be a friend of the world becomes an enemy of God" (James 4:4. See also James 1:27 and Romans 12:2).

But what do these Bible writers mean by the term "world?" It cannot indicate separation from the people of the world, for Paul said that would mean we would have to leave the physical world altogether (1 Cor 5:10). We have seen how Jesus befriended despised tax-gatherers and other sinners. The "world" from which we are to be separated is the system of rebellion and living our lives without God. The apostle John describes this evil world system in three ways and tells us to keep ourselves from it. Here are the three phrases he uses:

i) The lust of the flesh.

Lust in this context means participation in deeds of the body in excess. We all know, for example, that eating and drinking are not only legitimate, they are God-given pleasures in which we are to participate. However, we know that gluttony and drunkardness are sin. Sexual expression within marriage is another God-given joy (Prov. 5:18-23), but sexual relationships outside of God's limits, are wrong. And while Jesus taught us to come aside and rest awhile, laziness and excessive indulgence in the comforts and luxuries of a life of ease are against God's will. The average man in this world panders to his flesh too much. Instead of being the master of his body, his bodily appetites control him. If a person is really repentant, his desires to indulge in these lusts will change.

ii) The lust of the eyes.

This is covetousness, the great sin of the Western world, the great idol before which many white-skinned people bow daily. To be covetous is to be possession-oriented. The problem with this is that the more possession-oriented we are, the less people-oriented we are and the further we will be from the will of God. Covetousness is not only a sin but a part of the world system that we as Christians are to resist. Jesus spoke loud and clear on this issue. If He were on our planet today, he would possibly lift up His voice on Wall Street and cry, "A man's life does not consist in the abundance of the things he possesses" (Luke 12:15). A man's success as far as God is concerned, is not measured in possessions. Godly wealth is walking closely with the Lord and with those around us. By our lifestyle we must preach this message today.

In 1982, the average annual income per person throughout the Third World was US $200. In some countries like Haiti and Bangladesh it was a mere $100 a year. Although you get more for your money in the Third World, $200 even there, cannot begin to compare with what can be purchased with the average annual income in the United States or Europe. Someone has said that the lifestyle of the average American today is the equivalent of how the Caesars lived in the days of Christ. We certainly have enough, don't we? Let's not grieve God here. The Ten Commandments forbids covetousness (Ex. 20:17). So does the apostle Paul who actually called it idolatry (Col 3:5). And we know no idolater will make it to heaven (1 Cor. 6:10).

iii) The pride of life.

Simply stated, it is the desire to be worshipped. Now, most of us would never admit to thinking like that, but even so, that desire to elevate ourselves has to be constantly checked. It was what led the devil astray (Is. 14:12-15) and it is what led the Pharisees from the true path during the time of Christ (John 5:44). It has also led respected church leaders astray down through the centuries. It can be expressed in such non-obvious ways like criticizing someone else so our efforts look better. An even more subtle expression of it is the withholding of praise from those to whom it is due so that we don't compare unfavorably with them. The pride of life is the sin of entertaining selfish ambitious thoughts about

oneself and living for honor from others. It is totally
opposed to the way of humble trust in which Jesus
intended us to live. For many, the lust for power,
public esteem and prestige is more compelling than
the lust for money. Pride of life means living for
status and success. But these things should no longer
rule in a Christian's life.

The apostle John was inspired by the Holy Spirit
to define these areas as the spirit of the world. If our
lives are governed by these things, he warned, we are
at enmity with God.

3) We are required to turn from ourselves.

The apostle Paul points out that Jesus Christ died that we
should no longer live for ourselves, but live for Him who
died for us (2 Cor. 5:15). To not respond to Christ's
sacrificial love is unthinkable (Luke 14:26, Rom. 14:9).

4) We are required to turn from the devil.

According to Ephesians 2:2 we were all followers of the
devil until we came to Christ. The apostle John
re-emphasizes this concept when he writes that he who is
sinful is of the devil (1 John 3:8). Some will not feel that
they have been consciously living for the evil one, but at
the moment of repentance they should realize how much
they have served Satan's purposes for having not lived for
God. Obviously those who have dealt in black magic,
witchcraft and sorcery will be more aware of how they have
been in the devil's kingdom. They need to clearly
understand that Jesus Christ has power over Satan and
that Christ came specifically to destroy his works (Col.
2:15, Heb. 2:14, 1 John 3:8).

King Manasseh knew what it was like to serve Satan
and commit all sorts of atrocities against the Lord (2
Chron. 33:1-16). He practiced soothsaying, sorcery, dealt
with mediums and wizards, and even offered his children to
a foreign God. An idolater, he committed the hideous sin

of setting up a calf's image in the house of the Lord. God spoke to Manasseh but he refused to listen. Later army commanders from the king of Assyria took Manasseh, bound in chains to Babylon, where he finally humbled himself greatly before God. Deeply moved by this humbling, God restored Manasseh back to his kingdom. Once in Jerusalem again, Manasseh proved his contrition by amending his ways. He destroyed the foreign gods, removed the despicable image from the house of the Lord and restored godly worship to the temple. God is able to restore those who in humility turn to Him and turn their back on the devil and renounce his works.

I once shared the above story with a young man dressed in a black leather jacket at a Teen Challenge Center. He had been involved in black magic and was now reluctant to receive Christ. The devil had warned him that if he ever turned to God, satanic forces would be after him. I shared with him the verses that show that Christ's power is superior to the devil's (Col. 2:15, Heb. 2:14). He was amazed and relieved to know that Christ's power was greater. He confessed his sin of dealing in black magic and I rebuked the evil one. He then sat there awe-struck. After awhile he testified how his heart just burst with happiness. Such was his deliverance at that moment from the fear of the devil.

5) We are required to turn from idols.

In one sense, this has already been dealt with when we talked about turning from sin. In the three lists we mentioned earlier (Gal. 5:19-21, 1 Cor. 6:9-10, Rev. 21:8), each record idolatry as being one of those sins which, if found in a person's life, would prevent entrance into the kingdom of God. The Old Testament is full of God's commandments about not worshipping idols and his intense displeasure with those who did. It is incredible that people should deny the great God whom the heavens cannot contain, the God of limitless power and ingenuity, and worship before images made of gold, silver or stones

(Deut. 7:25-26, 1 Thess 1:9, Acts 17:25).

Many Christians are reluctant to say anything against idols, and I'm not suggesting that you should speak out against them during the early stages of your witnessing conversation. However, it is my view, that if a person indicates a desire to be saved, then it behooves us as servants of Christ to mention the need to forsake idols before even thinking about praying for them. Otherwise, it has the potential of leading to all sorts of frustrations at a later date. Besides, according to Scripture, real salvation cannot occur if the person does not turn from idolatry (Rev. 21:8). That verse reads, " . . . those who practice magic arts, the idolaters . . . their place will be in the fiery lake of burning sulfur."

By waiting until they have come this far in their understanding of the gospel, they should understand the necessity of forsaking idol worship. The apostle Paul had words of approval for the Christians of Thessalonica when he wrote, "They tell how you turned from *idols* to serve the living and true God, and wait for his son from heaven . . ." (1 Thess 1:9-10, emphasis added).

Those who have been habitual idol worshippers should be told that the devil often gives power to those idols being worshipped. That is all part of his scheme to keep people in the bondage of idolatry. Those coming to Christ need to know their authority in the Lord to be able to withstand any attack of the devil (Col. 2:15, Heb 2:14). But Satan will only flee from their rebuke after they have repented and have proved their repentance by destroying their idols. Repentance in this area is costly. When the Ephesians repented from their black magic, the value of the books they burned was the equivalent of 50,000 days wages (Acts 19:19). Modern day idolaters who come to Christ must likewise burn or break their idols. These idols must not be sold (no matter how much they are worth)— and they must not be given to others. That would only perpetrate the evil practice from which all are commanded to turn. The biblical pattern is to have them burned (Deut. 7:5, 25).

Counsel against the worshipping of ancestors should be discussed here, for this also comes in the category of idolatry. It is wrong for man to worship sinful man even if he is an ancestor, for the Bible prohibits worshipping any other than Deity (Acts 10:25-26, Acts 14:12-15). Even if an angel were to visit us, we would be forbidden to worship him (Rev. 19:10). If then, we are not allowed to worship God's perfect angelic creation, how much less is man fit to be given homage! "You shall have no other gods before me" is what we read in Exodus 20:3, and Jesus upheld this truth by declaring: "Worship the Lord your God and serve him only" (Matt. 4:10).

The above instruction needs to be given with considerable *gentleness* however, for it is not always easy for someone in five minutes, to drop beliefs that have been held for a life-time. In Chinese culture, for example, age is held in such great respect, that you can understand how easy it would be to become indoctrinated over the years to the concept of ancestral worship. While we must state the truths against the worship of ancestors, we must do it in such a sensitive way that we do not attack the non-Western practice of respecting one's elders. Many Western youth could take a lesson from this aspect of their culture. We must make sure the Third-Worlder doesn't believe that our instruction against ancestral worship is merely an extension of the disrespectful way many Westerners treat their elderly. Non-Westerners won't be so accepting of our teaching if we do. We must give them proper understanding between godly respect and ungodly worship.

There may be the need to warn those who have been involved in this practice of ancestral worship of the possibility of Satan's attacks, because they have now renounced it. But they also need to know the assurance that Christ's power is supreme over all, as they submit to Him (James 4:7).

6) We are required to turn from our careers if necessary.

Saul was a Jewish Rabbi who consented to the death of Christians and helped in their persecution. In his own words he was once a "blasphemer and a persecutor and a violent man" (1 Tim. 1:13). Saul could not continue in the religious system that was persecuting God's people. He had to give up his career as a Rabbi who was recognized by the Sanhedrin, a career for which he had trained many years. It meant going against the stream of human opinion. We are not told what his parents thought about him, but it could be he lost their respect as well. We are told that the Pharisees as a group loved money (Luke 16:14) and it is possible that Saul was well-heeled also. But he certainly knew what deprivation was after he turned to Christ. Saul had been an honored man and had outstripped many of his contemporaries during his rabbinical studies (Gal. 1:14). Immediately after he met the Lord however, he preached His gospel which led him into a life of often being despised and sometimes being beaten (2 Cor 6:9).

But it also meant he became the beloved apostle Paul, a man who has affected the world for Christ probably more than any other man during the history of the church. His conversion was dramatic. He was immediately open about his faith by preaching Christ in the synagogue in Damascus, the city of his conversion. He had immediate results as well. The Greek of Acts 9:25 reveals that it was his disciples (or converts) who let him down over the wall in a basket to safety when it was learned that there was a plot against his life. Yes, Paul's conversion meant a complete change of life for him.

Moses is another good example. Although he was enjoying the pleasure, comforts and luxuries of a palatial home in Egypt, he chose rather to suffer abuse with the children of God than to enjoy the pleasures of sin for a season (Heb. 11:25). What then, was his sin? The riches he was enjoying were the result of oppression. Pharaoh's household had forced the Hebrew people to labor in cruel conditions, and it was on the profits of their slavery that Moses was living. That meant that he was agreeing with this oppression. Thus he changed his mind.

Billy Graham once told the story of a man who owned a liquor store. He came to an evangelistic meeting and turned his life over to Christ. The next day the man went to his store, but not to trade. Instead, he hung a notice over the store which read, *"Out Of Business."* He has not been the only person to change his occupation in modern history. An Italian theater owner in Philadelphia once came to Christ and later, it was his turn to put up a sign over his business. In his expressive Italian English the big notice read, *"Closa Down On Accounta Salavation."*

These four illustrations show clearly the kind of repentance that God requires. It means the immediate linking of ourselves with the purposes of God. How different this kind of repentance is from many of the decisions that are registered for Christ today. It is a hope that this manual will encourage Christians to lead to Christ those who will indeed be like Caleb of old who "followed the Lord wholeheartedly" (Deut 1:36).

7) We are required to make restitution where necessary.

We must never lose sight of the fact that it is the sacrifice of Jesus Christ on the cross that provides the way back to God. But even so, God requires us to put right what we can, and thus to be reconciled to those whom we have hurt. Zacchaeus showed his repentance when he said he would give half of his goods to the poor and that if he had robbed any one, he would restore it four-fold (Luke 19:8). The Bible teaches we should pay back what we have stolen (Lev. 6:4-5, Ezek. 33:15, Matt 3:8, Acts 26:20).

I can remember quite clearly the things I stole from stores and other places during my unsaved days—cigarettes, packets of cookies, chocolate bars, socks, books and so on. I can also remember the letters of restitution I wrote during Bible College days and the checks I enclosed. One letter I wrote contained an apology for lying to the store owner who had suspected I had stolen a particular book. And I can still remember going with check in hand to the manager of Woolworths. For some reason, I had felt before God I was not to send it through the mail but go in person—probably because it was in that particular store I had been caught stealing as a twelve-year-old.

It is necessary for us to bear in mind that we cannot always make restitution for the things and lives we have damaged. How could a young man pay back the virginity he has robbed from a young lady? Obviously we cannot unscramble eggs. But even in such circumstances it would be fitting for the young man to deeply acknowledge his wrong and make sure any resultant child is being properly supported and prayed for. Not only does a Christian want to undo the damage that Satan is presently causing, he also wants to help to undo any damage he helped the devil do through his life before he came to Christ.

When things have become too cloudy to trace, there is always God to appeal to for wisdom. He will tell us what we should do. Don't worry about the things that don't bother you—but those that do bother you must be taken care of. Where details are hazy, He can always ask you to do something representative to put "that thing" right. But be prepared to humble yourself. And who knows? They might forgive you in which case you're free—you will not have to repay! In the case of my going to the manager of Woolworths, the manager would not accept my check. But I didn't really feel I was forgiven from a righteous base. The reason he would not receive my money was because he had stolen himself as a boy! In that particular instance I went around the corner and handed the money to a Christian organization. But that was my conviction. God may convince you quite differently.

I am reminded of the story of a young man whom we'll call Jack. He was a boat-builder by trade and had been wit-

nessing to his boss, but stealing special copper nails from
him at the same time. One day Jack's pastor preached a
message on the subject of restitution. Jack was convicted.
*My boss will think I am a hypocrite if I confess and put that
right,* he thought. *Yet I know what I must do!* Accordingly
the young man put the matter right.

His boss was moved. "I had considered you a
hypocrite but now I'm not sure." He went on to say that
any religion that moves someone to put a matter like this
right is worth looking into. We make restitution, of course,
to put things right with those we've offended, and not
preach. Yet it's interesting how often this act of obedience
makes people sit up and think seriously about the Lord
(and sometimes their own sin!).

Making restitution is a tangible proof of repentance.
The Bible teaches that repentance should be proved by the
lives that we lead (Matt. 3:8, Acts 26:20). John the Baptist
told the common people that if they were repentant they
would be generous and share: "The man with two tunics
should share with him who has none, and the one who has
food should do the same." He then proceeded to tell the
tax gatherers that the way they would prove their repentance was to be honest and forsake corruption, "Don't collect any more than you are required to." Lastly, he instructed the soldiers to show their repentance by forsaking
violence, being just and being content with their pay (Luke
3:8-14).

As we come towards the end of this subject on repentance, I should repeat that not everything mentioned here
needs to be said to the person on the street who is interested in salvation. However, the spirit of what is written
should be explained. But we must be careful about the
manner in which we say these things. If we sound cold, like
an unsympathetic magistrate, we will only testify against
the goodness of God who is just. God's commandments are
not burdensome (1 John 5:3). Sometimes we can be so
harsh and dogmatic that the unsaved will not sense the
grace of God. But then, we must not go to the other extreme of bringing God's justice into question by portraying

Him as sentimentally soft. God is gentle as we have already seen. But He still wants "rug-thumping" repentance. That's a deeper kind than is generally practiced today.

Chapter Thirteen

OTHER THINGS WE MUST DO

In the following pages we will discuss the other things we should tell the serious inquirer before leading him in a prayer for salvation. In addition to repenting, for example, our unsaved friend must:

1) Believe that Jesus is the only way.

In Chapter Eleven, we explained that only someone Divine could atone for our sins and be the means by which we have the opportunity for forgiveness. If you have been witnessing to someone along the suggested lines of this book, you have now come to the stage where your friend needs to acknowledge Christ is Lord to the exclusion of all others. This is going to be tough for some. Hindus, for example, believe all things are permissible, all gods are right and all paths lead to salvation. Therefore, the thing that will prove how close to the kingdom he is, will be whether he will acknowledge Jesus as Lord to the exclusion of *all* others he formerly called deities.

In Romans 10:9-10, the apostle Paul lays down one of the conditions to salvation. That is the belief that Jesus is Lord. That Scripture reads, " . . . if you confess with your mouth, Jesus is Lord, and believe in your heart that God raised him from the dead, you will be saved." For a Hindu to be saved he must acknowledge Jesus to be the Lord, not "lord" Ram, not "lord" Krishna, or any of the other gods. Many Hindus will be prepared to pray the sinner's prayer with us without any intention of getting rid of all their idols and other gods. They merely wish to add Jesus to the gods they already worship. This is because of the all-embracing, "all ways lead to God" philosophy of their religion. While we cannot pray with them when they are not of a biblically-based persuasion, we must keep up our love and non-condemning attitude toward them. We must patiently pray and trust that they will eventually place their faith exclusively in Jesus Christ.

Some may ask, "Aren't you being selfish to believe that Jesus is the only way to Heaven? What about Buddha, Confucius or Mohammed?" Let's then, compare these religious teachers with Christ and see if we are indeed being selfish or mean. The first question to ask ourselves is, "Did any of these three even claim to be God?" We know Buddha didn't, because he wasn't sure that there was a God. Confucius and Mohammed didn't either. In fact, Mohammed would have been very indignant if any had asked him if he were deity. To him, Allah alone was God.

Secondly, did any of these forgive sin? I am not aware that any claimed on their own merits to cleanse guilty people from their wrongdoing. Thirdly, did the leaders of the world's other major (or minor) religions ever rise from the dead? The answer is no, they didn't even claim to. But we have solid proof—the kind of proof that would stand up in court—that Jesus did.

Fourthly, do the leaders of the other world religions *radically* change lives for the better? For every one hundred prostitutes that Jesus Christ cleanses, how many devoted to Buddha undergo this kind of change? For every one hundred murderers that Christ changes, how many does Mohammed turn into men of love? And for every one hundred homosexuals or drug-addicts whom Christ changes, I wonder how many have been made new through the teachings of Confucius or Krishna?

In view of the above, I do not believe that we are

being selfish or unreasonable to believe that only Jesus is the way to God and that forgiveness of sins is to be found in Him alone. In the same way, we are not being unreasonable to believe that two and two equals four and that every day the tides go in and out. These are proven facts. So too, it is a belief in facts that lead us to intelligently follow Jesus Christ, the Son of the living God!

The Scripture is firm on this issue. Jesus' statement as recorded in John 14:6 was: "No one comes to the Father *except through me*." The apostle Peter put it this way: "Salvation is found in no one else, for there is *no other name* under heaven given to men by which we must be saved" (Acts 4:12). And the apostle Paul declared, "For there is one God and *one* mediator between God and men, the man Christ Jesus" (1 Tim. 2:5).

While we know that Jesus is the only way to heaven and while we must be uncompromising in our beliefs, it is absolutely important that our spirits must exhibit the character of Christ as we share these truths. Otherwise our "truth" becomes "untruth." In other words, the *facts* of the Scriptures must be said in a way that is consistent with the love and accepting *spirit* of the Son of God. Otherwise it will be harder for our words to be owned by the Holy Spirit, whose job it is to lead men into all truth (John 16:13).

This brings us to the next step our unsaved friend must take. He must:

2) Make Jesus Lord.

The apostle Paul and others were men who made Jesus the Lord of their lives. They are shining examples to us. Yet we must understand that to make Jesus the Lord of our lives is not an optional extra. The apostle Paul said it this way, "And he died for all, that those who live should no longer live for themselves but for him who died for them and was raised again." Submission to the loving Lordship of Christ is actually a natural outgrowth of having been lovingly wooed by Him. It should be reasonable to think that because of Jesus Christ's astonishing sacrifice for us, we would want to respond in love by yielding our lives to Him. Not that Jesus requires this of us for selfish reasons. He is thinking of our good, the welfare of the whole universe and how best public justice can be served. The most sensible thing we can do with our lives is to let Him control them. If we do, it will be the best for us, the best for our immediate community, and the best for the world at large.

Unless an inquirer is extremely prepared by God, it is my view that we should allow the inquirer a day or two to think all this over before committing himself to such a drastic change of lifestyle. If we are going to err in the timing of the sinner's prayer, I feel it is better to err on the side of caution than to urge a person into making a hurried, rash decision. When we lead someone to the Lord, we are leading him along an entirely different road from the one he has walked on for years. He'll have to have new and godly ambitions with new friends and maybe new enemies. If we do not lay the proper foundation, he is likely to have second thoughts at a later stage.

The importance of this step is significant when we realize that in the New Testament the word "Lord" appears well over 700 times. The word "Savior" on the other hand, is mentioned only 24 times, and then seldom is it used by itself—usually it is linked with "Lord" or some similar word. This is an indication to me where God wants the emphasis. The next step is to urge our friend to:

3) Witness for Christ.

The Scriptures indicate that we are to open our mouths and acknowledge that we belong to Jesus Christ. In fact, Jesus taught that salvation is conditional upon the acknowledging of the Son of God. This is a concept that Paul also was to declare (Rom 10:9-10). "Whoever acknowledges me before men," Jesus said, "I will also acknowledge him before my Father in heaven. But whoever disowns me before men, I will disown him before my Father in heaven" (Matt. 10:32-33). It is significant that we have been told as a body of believers to preach the gospel. This is, of course, in addition to letting our lives speak (Matt. 5:16). Someone had to open their mouths for us to hear the gospel.

Perhaps it is helpful to think back to the days when we were not Christians and to consider how our words made the world worse—even if it was just the world around us. Now, if we have really given our lives to Christ, we should desire to use our powers of speech to help people and make the world around us a better place. If Jesus said that out of the fullness of the heart the mouth speaks, then the proof of the conversion of our hearts will find expression through our lips. That will include sharing the Lord Jesus with others. Speaking is a proof of believing (2 Cor. 4:13).

****

This ends the subject of repentance and the other conditions necessary for salvation. We need not go into all the details that we have covered in the last two chapters, as this has mainly been given for our understanding of the subject. But it is important that we mention the essence of this teaching, and if we have, the inquirer now is in a position to pray.

For anyone who does want to follow Christ, it is good if he prays his own prayer out loud. The step will mean much more to him if he does. The ideal, of course, is to provide an opportunity in an atmosphere of love for the Holy Spirit to bring such conviction, whereby the sinner spontaneously cries out to God of his own accord. The whole purpose of the way in which Jesus was put to death was to provide the opportunity for this kind of response as we saw in Chapter Eleven.

Expositors usually find the first reference in the Bible to any doctrine of special interest. For this reason the reference in Acts 2:37 merits attention, because it is the first time we read of the disciples preaching the gospel after receiving the Great Commission. The reaction of those hearing their preaching should thus be of particular interest to us. Under the convicting power of the Holy Spirit, those listening cried out loud, "What shall we do?" That sounds like they were ready to be prayed for! Later in the book of Acts we read of the Philippian jailor who got down on his knees and cried, "What must I do to be saved?" (Acts 16:30).

I believe there is a great need in the world as the church goes into the 1990's to present the gospel in such a way to allow the full weight of the convicting power of both the *love* and *purity* of the Holy Spirit to fall. John Wesley is reported to have asked the following question to his disciples after they had returned from preaching: "Did anyone get saved or did anyone get mad?" Perhaps he was seeking for some evidence of the conviction of sin as a result of the preaching of his followers.

The experience of C. H. Spurgeon (later to become known as the "Prince of preachers") is worthy of note. At the age of 14 the Holy Spirit came upon him in convicting power, even though he had been a moral person by today's standards. He was not like the other boys of his age who were untruthful, dishonest and swearing. Yet on that particular day, Spurgeon saw *how outrageous his sin was against God.* The majesty of God and Spurgeon's sinfulness filled him with penitence. There is no doubt about one thing. To the degree there is a real brokenness over sin, to that degree there will be lasting spiritual life.

That was certainly true in Spurgeon's life. Just five years after the deep dealings with God just mentioned, Spurgeon, at the age of 19, was preaching to crowds of 5,000. His critics said he would burn out and drop like a falling star. But he didn't. He continued to serve God faithfully to become the "prince of preachers" who led many to righteousness. It is interesting that he had no "altar calls," for he told his audiences that he would be in his study if people wanted to talk to him.

The interesting thing about this is that we have been mentioning conversions that took place without any hint of an "altar call" or a plea to "come forward" by a persuasive evangelist. In fact, "altar calls" were unheard of until Charles Finney introduced them last century. But then we understand why Finney did so. He gave people the opportunity to respond to these calls *only* after they had been under conviction for days, if not weeks.

Deep dealings with God produce results. Charles Finney had lasting fruit from his "slow" methods of evangelism. I am told that after a series of meetings in Rochester, New York, a total of 100,000 came to the Lord. Ten years later, 80 percent of those converts were still standing, and the bars and drinking saloons were still closed. The challenge is always the following: "How do we provide the Holy Spirit the opportunity to bring conviction in the atmosphere of love and not condemnation?" That is the question that faces each one of us.

There will be times, though, when you will feel you need to guide people in how to pray. The following things could be shared with them as things they could mention to God in prayer. 1) They have willfully done wrong to hurt God and others; 2) they are now going to turn from everything they know is wrong and ask for God's forgiveness; 3) they are going to ask God for grace to overcome the power of sin in their lives; 4) they are now submitting themselves to the Lordship of Christ and will take sides with God to fight against evil in the world; and 5) they will read the Bible, pray, fellowship with other Christians and openly testify about our Lord Jesus Christ.

It is my suggestion before you say "Amen" at the end of your prayer, that you linger on with head bowed, praying silently that God would confirm things to the person who has just prayed. This is a hallowed moment which is sometimes spoiled by immediate talking. Allow the Holy Spirit to speak to the new Christian's heart, bringing assurance, instruction and even further conviction.

Even if you did not lead people to Christ, it is also my suggestion that you endeavor to pray with them before you leave. Obviously you will not pray the sinner's prayer, but you can pray with them that God would help them understand the message you just brought. After prayer, apply the same method of allowing God to speak to their hearts by the Holy Spirit. Don't linger on too long. It is interesting just how often, when you do lift your head with an "Amen," that you'll notice them wiping a tear away from their eyes. They will have been touched by God's Spirit, maybe for the first time in their lives. This may be because you will have been the first person in communion with God whom they have ever heard pray. Their hearts will be softer the next time you, or someone else, revisits them.

Actually I have an interesting story to relate here. It was the day after I met Kuhammed, the young Kuwaiti I talked to on the flight from Colombo mentioned in Chapter Six. I was in Hong Kong and, as I took a taxi to Kai Tak Airport, I excitedly prayed. I thanked the Lord in faith for the person He was going to place beside me on this Philippine Airline flight to Manila.

Climbing on board after check-in, I discovered my assigned seat on the Airbus placed me in a two-seats-only-together circumstance, just ideal for a witnessing situation. A young Filipina called Juanita sat by the window. As we got talking, I found out she was from Baguio, the very city Margaret and I had formerly lived in for ten very happy years. Juanita was now returning home—fleeing from a cruel employer in the Crown Colony. She was fearful, wondering how her parent's would react to her sudden reappearance at home when they had helped her financially to get to Hong Kong to find work in the first place. In God's perfect timing he placed me in a position to alleviate those fears. You might say I met her *felt* need. But my big point in relating this story is simply this. I didn't "lead her" to Christ. Although she had been listening and we'd enjoyed a good time of talking together, she didn't give me the impression she was wanting to give her life over to God. I simply asked if I could pray a general prayer. It was the kind I mentioned above—the type we attempt to pray even with those who don't respond or who are not ready to respond.

Two years passed. True, we had written to each other once and I had even seen her briefly in a meeting in

Baguio on one occasion. But the thing that surprised me—two full years after that Philippine Airline flight, was a letter from Juanita and her friend. Reference was made in it about my leading her to Christ on that flight. I puzzled over that for a couple of months until a friend shared the following. "We come to Christ," he said, "when we say *yes* to God, not when someone prays a sinner's prayer." Or goes forward or signs a decision card for that matter. That really makes sense.

But then, so does the opposite thought—how many people do we see praying the sinner's prayer and yet they never say *yes* to God in their hearts?

So, by all means, pray a general prayer about God leading them into truth, about helping them understand the things you have shared, about blessing their families, and healing their sick, etc. Although they may never pray after us, they may well be saying yes to God—at least in the sense that they'll start doing some thinking about what we've shared. This is a very good reason why we should revisit interested contacts—but then we're getting ahead of ourselves.

In the next chapter we will explain further why it is so necessary to take this slower and more sure route in leading people to our blessed Lord.

Chapter Fourteen

COUNTING THE COST

It is possible, after having read the foregoing chapters that you may say to yourself, "I don't think we have to be as careful as that before we lead people in a sinner's prayer." I can certainly understand your feeling that way. The best answer I have is to simply examine Jesus' discourse in Luke 14:25-35 and trust that it will shed further light on this important subject.

These verses tell of the time when a large crowd followed Jesus one day. The sheer size of the group in itself would have pleased the Lord, for we know He wants all to be saved (1 Tim. 2:4, 2 Pet. 3:9). At the same time, however, Jesus must have suspected that the loyalty of those who were following Him was somewhat shallow. Stopping to address them, He therefore stated His terms of discipleship.

"If anyone comes to me," Jesus started, "and does not hate his father and mother, his wife and children, his brothers and sister—yes, even his own life—he cannot be my disciple" (verse 26). The use of a contrast to indicate a comparison is a Hebrew way of teaching, and therefore must be interpreted within that cultural parameter. Jesus was simply saying, "Anyone who loves his father or mother more than me is not worthy of me; anyone who loves his son or daughter more than me is not worthy of me" (Matt.

10:37). It appears that Jesus, keen as He was on numbers, was declaring that quality was to come before quantity. We are to love our families, of course, for this is godly (Ex. 20:12, Eph. 5:25, 6:4). But when there comes a choice of loyalties between them and God, we must choose to put Him first.

This has to be sensitively and lovingly pointed out to non-Westerners whose strong family-orientation tendencies we have already mentioned. It is only before God that we will appear on the day of judgment—not our relatives. Loving God more than family, however, was only one part of the commitment Jesus stated He wanted from His listeners. He proceeded to add another: "And anyone who does not carry his cross and follow me cannot be my disciple" (verse 27).

When Jesus said these words, He was again talking within a specific cultural setting—that of Palestine at the time of the Romans. Anyone carrying a cross in those days had been given the death sentence by crucifixion, and hundreds had been put to death in this fashion. If Jesus were on earth here in America today he would have to say, "Unless you are prepared to go to the electric chair, or be gassed, you cannot be my disciple."

To "carry a cross" then, meant being dead to pride and personal ambition. It meant receiving insults and sneers. But even more important, it meant this: If you're to follow Jesus, you need to be prepared to follow Him even to death. Otherwise, Jesus said, "you cannot be my disciple."

It is interesting therefore, that Jesus did not recruit by picturing a rosy one-sided view of what it meant to follow Him. He was honest, and I feel that we need to remember His example here and not promise "the moon" to a potential convert if he will only come to Christ. While joy and forgiveness should be his portion, the promise that no more problems will come his way should not be given. He is actually likely to have more problems in some areas because he will now be a threat to the kingdom of darkness!

Many times we are tempted to think we need to hide

the fact that certain renunciations will be required of a would-be convert if he comes to Christ. We feel afraid he might not come to the Lord if he knows too much. But I well remember making an interesting observation many years ago when I was living in the Philippine city of Baguio.

Our YWAM team had been out witnessing among the people that day and had invited folks to hear me speak that night. I had chosen as my sermon, the story of Zacchaeus, which lends itself to the question of restitution. Unknown to me, one of our team members had brought into the meeting a former gang leader. This young man called Archie and his companions had stolen frequently. One of their pastimes had been the smashing of car windows and the stealing of stereo equipment from inside those cars. One night he and his companions had broken into a department store and had stolen merchandise which they later resold. With the money they obtained in this fashion, they then proceeded to have a big party on one of the sandy beaches down the mountain from the city. You would think that a message on paying back what you'd stolen would be the last thing that would attract a gang leader to the gospel.

But Archie came back for more and heard me speak on yet another occasion. The Ywammer who had first contacted him continued to befriend him, and Archie subsequently came to the Lord. Later, I shared this story with Loren Cunningham, expressing my surprise that a gang leader who had so much to put right, would respond to a message on restitution. But Loren didn't seem amazed at all. I well remember his reply: "Archie felt guilty, and you gave him the opportunity to come out from beneath that load. That's why he responded."

And Archie meant business with the Lord. He moved into the YWAM house and joined us. Whenever he could, he got himself hired for the day and worked, recording the comings and goings of a group of Baguio's jeeps used for public transportation. Faithfully he brought home pesos he earned, and of his own volition he would then hand the money to one of our team members for safe keeping. (He felt this was best—otherwise the money might get spent!) When an amount had been reached sufficient to pay back someone he had wronged, he would then make the necessary restitution. Archie is now with the Lord, having lost his life in a swimming accident while on a Christian outreach. I'm sure, if he knew, he would be delighted that his testimony is being used here. I can just see the smile on his face! The object in telling his story is this: Knowing he would be required to pay back what he had stolen did not keep him from coming to the Lord.

I also believe it is only honest to give people *time* to think about what is going to be involved in becoming a Christian. Jesus implied this by the story he gave to the crowds that day.

"Suppose one of you wants to build a tower," Jesus continued. "Will he not first sit down and estimate the cost to see if he has enough to complete it?" Likewise, a person coming to Christ needs to sit down and contemplate, "Once I become a Christian, am I going to continue being one, despite the cost involved?" I believe we as evangelists need to give people the opportunity to think these things through.

After giving the above illustration, Jesus continued by giving another, this time about a king wanting to go out to war with only half the number of troops that the opposing army had. "Will he not first sit down and consider whether he is able?" Jesus asked.

The thing that is common to both stories is this: The person confronted with the decision *sat down first* and considered the cost, before he *rose up to act*. We must allow our contacts to do the same.

But there is one more aspect of these parables we need to consider. In this second story of Jesus, the king had only half the soldiers that his enemy had. I believe it was no coincidence that Jesus used this particular illustration. He wanted to emphasize that when we become a Christian, we are out of step with the majority of the population. Would-be converts need to be aware of this when they make their decision.

Margaret and I once heard John Stott, the noted author on evangelism speak in Hong Kong. At the time, Rev. Stott was preaching on his series of evangelistic messages entitled, "The Revolution of Jesus Christ." I will never forget what he said one evening before he closed the meeting. On that occasion he gave the opportunity for people to become Christians, in what I would consider a different yet thoroughly appropriate manner. He announced that those who wanted to come to Christ were to come to the front to talk to him. But he announced that he would be dismissing the meeting first.

"In this way," he said, "you will have to fight against the crowd in order to reach me." Then he continued, "That will be a good introduction to how it will be once you become a Christian. You'll be fighting against the tide the rest of your life!"

I certainly appreciated his sentiments. After all, people want to know what is ahead of them before they sign up for a job, build a house or agree to a new car. They feel terribly cheated if information is withheld from them.

This is one reason, I believe, that when it comes to "signing someone up" to be a Christian, we have to be even more careful that we are not withholding information that they need. Let's not fear to let people know the terms of discipleship that Jesus laid down. Actually, I believe one of the reasons why some don't follow the Lord is because we *do* withhold information concerning terms of discipleship. As a consequence the sinner says, "That's too easy!"

And I believe they are right!

Just one word of caution. People can take all sorts of rules and restrictions if the person stating them has a soft spirit. But if we appear metallic and harsh, they will not be attracted to Christ, for we will not be exhibiting the character of God. The terms on which Jesus accepts the sinner are not the easiest—the Bible doesn't promise that. They are, however, the very best that God could offer. In fact, the angels are awed by what has been given into our hands (1 Pet. 1:10-12).

Let's make sure then, that we state all the above terms in the most Christ-like spirit possible.

III. PRESERVING THE RESULTS

Chapter Fifteen

FOLLOW-UP

To my mind, there are two kinds of follow-up. The first is revisiting those who have not yet come to Christ. They are however, people whom God impresses us to revisit, for the Lord is moving in their hearts. Many times this kind of follow-up results in someone coming to Christ like the Sri Lankan Banker mentioned in the first chapter.

The second type is the revisiting of those who have already made a commitment to Christ. This is the kind we will mostly be concerned with here. Following up those who have come to Christ can be the most rewarding and exciting aspect of evangelism. To see the new Christian making strides to live a life of holiness and tell others about Christ is thrilling! However, some may remember their experiences in this area and recall how frustrating and unrewarding it all was. This can often be the case if care was not taken to make sure that the inquirer was really ready to come to Christ in the first place. Unless time was taken *then* to explain the terms of discipleship that Jesus gave, it's possible to go back to visit the "new Christian" and find that he is no longer interested. This is indeed heartbreaking.

Even when care has been taken to do things correctly, the need for follow-up still exists. The new Christian often needs much guidance, encouragement and even protection in some locations. In countries where there is hostility to Christianity, conversion can mean total rejection and persecution, even by members of the immediate family. The apostle Paul was smuggled out of a city in a basket down a wall in the dead of night soon after his conversion, you may remember (Acts 9:23-25). Being group-oriented, as we saw earlier, the Third-Worlder will not find it easy to survive spiritually by himself. He will need to belong to a new group—the loving body of Christ in a tangible small-group setting. Ideally, he will need to have the security of knowing that this group to which he is now a part, will continue to exist for a long time.

Even in a peaceful non-persecution Western setting, the need for follow-up still remains. Let's look for a minute at the ministries of two outstanding preachers of the 1700's—John Wesley and George Whitfield—to understand this concept more fully.

John Wesley made it his policy to organize his converts into societies and to appoint leaders over them, so that they would be adequately instructed and trained in righteousness. On the other hand, George Whitfield had no such follow-up plan. He was however, a man of considerable anointing who moved people in his day by the power of his preaching. On one occasion, he spoke to a crowd of 30,000 from the steps of a windmill without the aid of a microphone. Coalminers with soot-begrimed faces wept, their tears leaving tracks down their blackened cheeks. But just before his death he felt that it had not been enough. He is reported to have made the comment that in comparison with the *lasting* fruit of John Wesley's ministry, he had merely "knitted a rope of sand." That was no mean statement. Not all evangelists however, are called to form a denomination. Even so, Whitfield obviously felt he had been insufficient in the realm of follow-up.

What then, can we learn from the Bible about this subject? In his first letter to the church in Thessalonica, the apostle Paul gave some guidelines about this aspect of evangelism. Firstly, he encourages us with the concept that the lasting fruit of our labor is our reward. He called those, whom he had led to Christ, his "crown of rejoicing" (1 Thess. 2:19). Paul coined this term, thinking of the trophy that athletes at the Olympic Games received if they were victorious. We would do well to pause here and just reflect for a moment. If Jesus Christ were to return to earth right now, how many of the people we had led to the Lord or had helped bring to Him, would be our "crown of rejoicing?" This is quite a thought.

It is very encouraging to see our converts standing strongly for the Lord. "For now we really live," wrote Paul, "since you are standing firm in the Lord" (1 Thess. 3:8). The healthy spiritual state of the believers comforted Paul in his trials and affliction. "In all our distress and persecution," he wrote, "we were encouraged about you because of your faith" (1 Thess. 3:7).

The work of the Lord can get discouraging at times, but it is so stimulating to know that it is really worthwhile when you can think of those whom you have led to the Lord who are remaining true to God. This is one of the rewards for taking the slower route in evangelism, rather than the "let's have results quickly" approach.

But let's look at the aspect of follow-up itself. Is there really a key to this activity? I believe there is. It is the *motive* with which we serve God in the first place. If our heart is not in our witnessing, then it is unlikely that our hearts will be in doing follow-up either. To the degree we are faithful in the first aspect of evangelism, to that degree we are likely to be effective in the second. We have to realize that it is possible to witness because of a sense of duty, not love, or because we want to impress others or for some other reason. The proof of this is often revealed in the sometimes shocking lack of interest in follow-up. Some Christians have never bothered to revisit open-hearted people who could be encouraged towards following the Lord. This is such a shame!

But not so the apostle Paul. His witness was from the heart. "We were delighted to share with you not only the gospel of God but our *lives* as well, because you had been so dear to us" (1 Thess. 2:8). That, my friend, is witnessing from the heart. Sincere, warm, unselfish giving of ourselves is costly and should be a mark of every Christian. If we're going to be effective—especially in the non-Western World, it is important to have a heart like the one described in the verses just mentioned above.

Paul's heartfelt concern for his Thessalonian converts led him to do three things in the realm of follow-up which can be an example to us:

1) Paul revisited his converts when he could.

The Book of Acts is a testimony to the fact that Paul revisited his converts. In fact, his primary motive in undertaking the *second* Missionary Journey was to revisit those he and Barnabas had led to Christ on their *first* trip (Acts 15:36).

But it's his second missionary journey that we want to talk about now. During this trip, Paul preached to the Thessalonians and won a number of them to the Lord. Later he wanted to revisit them as well, but was hindered by his hostile opponents who had previously run him out of town. Paul was not the kind of person, however, to just shrug his shoulders and do nothing. His heart was for the Thessalonians for whom he cared deeply. Thus, when he was unable to return, he sent Timothy to exhort and establish them (1 Thess. 3:1-2). It must be remembered that his *desire* was to return himself, and I believe that is our first principle in follow-up. If that is not possible, then great efforts should be made to send someone else.

This brings us to an important question: What do we do at the end of a short-term outreach in a non-Western country in which we have been involved? How do we visit them when we may now be halfway around the globe? Do we send someone? My answer to that question is based on my observations in the Third World where I have lived most of my adult life. I feel it is important in these countries to introduce our converts to a permanent loving group as soon as possible after their conversion. If the converts get bonded in tightly with the short-term team and not with a permanent group, then unnecessary tearing occurs in the souls of the local converts when it is time for the short-termers to leave. The reason for this is because of the group- and interaction-orientation of the non-Westerner. The result can be hurtful both to them and to the advancement of the kingdom of God in that location. This means a certain amount of sacrifice on the part of the short-termer who leads people to the Lord in that segment of the world. Obviously we want to spend time with our spiritual children. And that we can do as long as they get bonded more with the permanent group than with us. (Better still, we could always plan to stay in that country for the next ten years!) To summarize this first principle: *Converts have to have personal contact with Christians nearby who care.*

2) Paul labored in prayer for his converts.

It seemed that the great apostle was not content to have people join Christ's cause and then not mature. He travailed in prayer that Christ be formed in them (Gal. 4:19). Without ceasing, he remembered Timothy in prayer night and day when Timothy was a pastor in Ephesus (2 Tim: 1:3-4). Paul wrote of Epapthras as one who labored fervently in prayer all the time for the Christians who had been subjected to heresy at Colosse. Epapthras prayed that these Christians might be mature and stand firm in the will of God (Col. 4:12).

There was once a missionary who worked among the Lisu people in the Southwestern hill country of China near the Burmese border. The time came when he had to leave them due to a war that was going on in the area. Although he was separated from them geographically—he was not in spirit. He prayed for them daily while at the same time working in the lowlands. Then, after two years, the situation changed enough to be able to visit the Lisu people in the hills again. There he noticed something interesting—the Lisu believers had grown more spiritually in his absence as a result of his prayers, than those with whom he had been working down on the plain!

What do we mention in prayer then, when we pray for those who have come to the Lord? We should stand in prayer between them and Satan, and resist his attacks on their lives and minds and as they face temptation. Prayer can be offered that they would love the fellowship of the saints which is of utmost importance. Naturally we should pray that they in turn would witness well to others. One person coming to the Lord can often open the door for many relatives and friends to get saved too—especially in non-Western countries. This is an extremely important subject and deserves far more space that we will give it here. Missiologists call it *networking*. When one person comes to Christ, they immediately have an open door to reach a number of people that they can influence in that special just-after-they-have been-converted period of time. These include family members, siblings, cousins, neighbors and friends, especially in Third-World nations where people live in such close proximity to each other. It is not uncommon to see many come to Christ like this in a short space of time. We should pray for it, encourage it for all we are worth and expect it to happen.

A good New Testament illustration of this is when the woman at the well excitedly ran back to her town saying, "Come see a man who told me everything I ever did!" Many of her townspeople believed in Jesus as a direct result of the woman's enthusiastic testimony. But it didn't stop there. The locals urged Jesus to stay with them. So Jesus did for two days and the movement grew. Because of Jesus' ministry in the town "many more became believers as well" (John 4:39-42).

We must pray then, for new converts. But we also need to pray for those dear people we've contacted who have not yet yielded their lives to Christ, that God will bring our words back to their remembrance and that they would seek honestly after God. I believe a wonderful opportunity for the gospel is sadly lost when we don't pray for those to whom we have just witnessed or preached. After a

Christian has lovingly witnessed to an unbeliever, the Holy Spirit has so much more to work with than before. He can now impress upon their heart and conscience the words we have spoken and the love we gave them. How thrilling to see folk saved as a result of prayer (1 Cor. 9:10). Our second principle in follow-up therefore is that *we must pray* for those we have witnessed to, especially for those whom we have led to Christ.

3) Paul wrote letters.

Paul's letters to the Thessalonians are a lasting testimony that he sat down and wrote letters to exhort and instruct them. If there had been telephones, telex-machines, and such things as audio and video-cassettes, he would have used these to encourage and instruct his converts as well. It can become costly sending books and tapes through the mail. But that's just the outworking of the "sharing our lives" concept which the apostle wrote about (I Thess. 2:7-8). Our third principle therefore, is that *we should communicate,* using all the things we have mentioned here.

In the realm of being an effective witness and successful in the ministry of follow-up, we should realize that our spare time can be used in the thrilling and rewarding pursuit of spending time with new babes in Christ, just as a mother delights in spending time with each of her newborn. To inspire you further about the subject of follow-up, I would encourage you to read the entire book of 1 Thessalonians.

In the next chapter we will discuss the things we should teach new converts on these follow-up visits.

Chapter Sixteen

INSTRUCTIONS FOR NEW CONVERTS

Just as it was important to spend time with the unconverted, carefully outlining the things necessary for salvation, so it is of equal importance that we spend time with the "newborn babies" in Christ (1 Pet. 2:2). Everything looks straightforward to us, but to the young Christian, it is not always like that. The questions he has may seem trivial to us, but they could be of utmost importance to him.

There are five main subjects the new convert should be taught immediately. We should go over these points briefly after someone has come to Christ, but obviously the newly saved is not going to be able to retain everything in one day. It is suggested therefore, that on revisits these points should be more thoroughly explained. Here then, are the five subjects:

1) The necessity of prayer.

At the heart of Christianity is communion with God. One of the reasons we know we are saved is the fact that we have this fellowship with Him. Jesus Christ defined salvation for all by saying that Eternal Life was knowing

God and Jesus Christ whom He had sent (John 17:3). We must then, encourage our newly-converted friends to maintain this fellowship with God at all costs. It is interesting that when Jesus taught His disciples to pray (Matt. 6:9-13), He gave them a pattern that encouraged them to enter into a time of prayer by praising God instead of diving to their knees and immediately presenting their "shopping list" of things they wanted. Jesus inferred that we should first unhurriedly worship and reverence Him. Such a notion is contained in His words, "Hallowed be your name" at the beginning of his discourse.

The next part of the prayer is, "Your kingdom come. Your will be done on earth as it is in heaven." Here, Jesus is instructing his disciples to pray for others. This means to pray for people to be saved, for Christians to be strengthened and for righteousness to rule in men's hearts. The new convert should be taught to pray for the salvation of his family and those to whom he has born witness. He should also be exhorted to remember his Christian brothers in prayer.

Jesus' pattern of prayer then, encourages the Christian to pray for himself and his needs such as his daily food, clothing, and shelter (verse 11). He is also encouraged to pray about his spiritual needs, like extending forgiveness to others (verse 12). I can hardly over-emphasize this aspect of the prayer. It has been the lack of a forgiving spirit that has spelled spiritual ruin to so many who otherwise would have risen to do great things for God and His kingdom. If you want your friend to remain in Christ and be effective, this truth of forgiving others has to be stressed. To keep on forgiving (and forgiving!) is one of the key ways to keep spiritually healthy. It is only logical that if we are going to represent Christ's willingness to forgive the sins of the un-saved, then our lives have to be representative of this forgiving spirit. So important is this truth that Jesus reinforces this principle by declaring later, "But if you do not forgive men *their* sins, your father will not forgive *your* sins" (Matt. 6:15).

The Christian should continually pray to hate sin more

and thus become more conformed to the image of Christ (Rom. 8:29). Notice that in the pattern given thus far, the order of prayer that Jesus gave us has been God first, others second and self last. This of course, should be the mark of a Christian. I once heard John Stott say that sin is the reversing of this order. The sinner puts self first, others second (when it suits him) and God last, or not at all. It is interesting that Jesus ended His pattern of prayer for His disciples to follow by saying, "For yours is the kingdom and power and the glory for ever. Amen." That certainly is a fitting way to end a time with the Lord.

2) The importance of the Bible.

Once the newly converted has confidence in the authenticity of the Bible, we should explain how essential it is for our spiritual well-being. It is also good for a new convert to be introduced very early to the understanding that the Bible is the highest court of appeal to the Christian. In the Book of Acts we have an example of just how this "appeals court" worked. The apostle Paul, during his travels, spoke in a Jewish Synagogue in the Macedonian town of Berea in what is now Northern Greece. The Jews were very interested in the apostle's message, but they wanted to check it out against the Word of God before committing themselves to follow his teaching. Acts 17:11-12 reads, "Now the Bereans received the message with great eagerness and *examined* the Scriptures every day to see if what Paul said was true." We will be giving our new converts a valuable tool if we teach them to compare every teaching they hear with the overall tone of the Bible. A knowledge of the Scriptures is a way of safeguarding us all from unbiblical principles and even unscriptural emphasis.

In some cultures, you may find it necessary to show the new Christian the passage in 2 Timothy 3:15-17, especially the words "from infancy you have known the Holy Scriptures . . . . " This is because some teach that we cannot understand the Bible even as an adult. Yet Paul here indicates that Timothy had known the Scriptures from childhood. Some also teach that tradition has more authority than the Bible. Jesus warned however, that it is possible to make the Word of God ineffective by our tradition (Mark 7:9,13; Matt. 15:3,6). Even though we know that not all tradition is wrong, Jesus came out very strong on the authority of the Word of God and charged the religious elders of His day with error because they did not know the Scriptures (Matt. 22:29). Jesus gave instruction that the Scriptures should be searched (John 5:39). He also said that heaven and earth will pass away but His Word will never pass away (Matt. 24:35).

3) The importance of a holy life.

Instruct the new convert to read the Bible at least once a day, for as food is to the body, so is Scripture to our soul and spirit. Someone has drawn the analogy between the Bible, which is called the "milk of the Word" (1 Pet. 2:2) and the milk of a mother. Just as the mother passes her immunizations against diseases to her newborn through the breast-feeding process, so too the receiving of the knowledge of the Word of God mightily helps us resist the forces of temptation that come against us.

In his excellent book *My Friend The Bible*, John Sherrill gives us some excellent advice on overcoming temptation. He encourages us to memorize verses of Scripture that we can quote to ourselves (or the devil) during times of temptation. Christians, he says, should recognize in what areas of their lives they are the weakest and have appropriate Bible verses ready to quote when those temptations arise. I would highly recommend that you read this book and even give copies to those you lead to Christ.[1] Explanation should also be given as to what the new Christian should do if he sins (1 John 1:9). That Scripture reads, "If we confess our sins, he is faithful and just and will forgive us our sins and purify us from all unrighteousness." There is cleansing in the blood of Christ.

4) The necessity of fellowshipping with other Christians.

As you witness, you will often hear the comment that we can be good Christians without going to church. The Bible teaches that once we belong to Christ we also belong to the body of believers world-wide whom God calls "the church." I believe it would be very helpful to teach the concept very quickly that the new Christian has certain responsibilities to discharge to this body of believers. Each one of us has a role to play in this group of believers as we exercise our God-given gifts and callings. Each Christian also has the privilege to receive from this body inspiration, instruction, correction and the encouragement of fellowship.

In practical terms, much of the above takes place within the context of a local body of believers who gather at regular intervals. Whether they meet in a cathedral or a jungle clearing makes no difference as far at its legitimacy is concerned in God's eyes, as long as the believers love God. The Scriptures encourage us, "Let us not give up meeting together, as some are in the habit of doing . . ." (Heb. 11:25). But it is not just attendance that God is looking for. If we have been touched by the sacrifice of Christ on Calvary, we should *want* to relate to a body of believers in a practical way beyond just warming a pew. "You are the body of Christ," Paul told the Corinthian Christians, "and each of you is a part of it" (1 Cor. 12:27).

Ideally the new convert should be a part of a group that provides spiritual fellowship, spiritual food and spiritual leadership. It should be a gathering of believers who practice righteousness and who have a vision to reach those who are unsaved. We should have sufficient confidence in our leaders so that we will be able in good conscience to fulfill the Scripture: "Obey your leaders and submit to their authority. They keep watch over you as men who must give an account. Obey them so that their work will be a joy, not a burden . . ." (Heb. 13:17). We may not have a gathering near us that answers to the description just given. In these circumstances, God would have us find a fellowship that is as close as possible to the description above.

5) The importance of witnessing to others.

This should be relatively easy for you to do because you have already given him an example of witnessing by having lead him to the Lord. Example is always the best teacher. Otherwise, if we tell people to do things we are not doing ourselves, the message they will receive is "what they say is really not very important."

If you have followed the pattern set down in this book, you will have already explained how confessing Christ to others is a condition of salvation. And if you have been witnessing for the glory of God, there must be a desire in your heart to see the world around you won to Christ. Enlist this new convert in the battle to turn the world to God. Encourage him at every turn, yet guide him too. A new convert is often high in zeal but often low on wisdom. However, if you channel his enthusiasm correctly, you might be able to achieve things you'll be amazed at. Endeavor to go witnessing with this new Christian, and pour into him the truths that you know and put books into his hands that will help him. Pray and fellowship with him, for in this way you'll be discipling him and multiplying your own ministry at the same time.

You may desire to give instruction on only one of these points each time you visit. But make sure that teaching on these four basic subjects be given as soon as possible.

---

1. John Sherrill, "My Friend The Bible," (Lincoln, VA., Chosen Books, 1978).

IS THE BIBLE INSPIRED?

Our purpose here is to outline ten simple reasons why the Bible can be trusted and why our faith can be placed in its teachings. We mentioned previously that some may desire to prove the Scriptures to be God's Word very early in conversation with the atheist, agnostic, Buddhist, Hippie, Moslem, Hindu, etc. Once the listener is convinced of the Bible's authenticity, it is a very powerful tool to use. It is important for us to realize however, that simply quoting 2 Timothy 3:16: "All Scripture is inspired by God . . . " is not objective proof to the non-Christian as to the Bible's divine origin. That proof must come from sources outside the Bible. What then, are the proofs that we can use?

The following are ten reasons for claiming the inspiration of the Bible. They are given with only a little explanation, although pages could be written on each reason.

1) Historical documents prove the Bible.

The NIV Study Bible lists 39 Ancient Texts that are examples of ancient non-Biblical documents. These 39 texts are just the major ones that provide information similar to various Old Testament passages or shed light on them. Inscriptions, for example, have been found that

vividly describe the desperate days preceding the siege of
Jerusalem by Nebuchadnezzar, the Babylonian king in
588-586 B.C.—a siege that is mentioned in Jeremiah 34.[1]
The historians Pilo, Eusebius, Josephus and others,
together with Jewish sacred writings, record things parallel
to the testimony of the New Testament writers. Historians
attest the accuracy of the list of government and religious
rulers in power in Palestine during the fifteenth year of
Tiberius Caesar, which is mentioned in Luke 3:1-2.

2) Archaeology upholds the testimony of Scripture.

Dr. Nelson Gluech, an outstanding Jewish archaeologist, in
his book, *Rivers in the Desert*, has made the remarkable
statement that no archaeological discovery has ever
contradicted the Bible. Examples of how archaeology
confirms Bible statements abound. Archaeologists have
uncovered numerous coins, writings and city sites which
have confirmed the Biblical record. For example,
archaeologists have uncovered evidence to the existence of
Lysanias the Tetrarch of Abilene (Luke 3:1-2). Before this
discovery, skeptics had considered Luke's reference to
Lysanias to be in error.

The accuracy of Luke's pen was also confirmed in
1961 by a team of Italians who unearthed an important in-
scription bearing the name of Pontius Pilate as they ex-
cavated in Caesarea. The stone calls Pilate "Prefect,"
which corresponds to Luke's term of "Governor." (Later,
Rome's ruler of the Judean Province were not called
Governors but Procurators.) One other example we'll
mention in passing.

John Garstang, between 1929 and 1936, made excava-
tions at the site of the city of Jericho, the first city captured
by the incoming Israelites under Joshua (Joshua 6).
Garstang found evidence that the city had been destroyed
suddenly because the grain bins were full and there was
plenty of food. He also found evidence from charred
remains, and the broken down walls that the city had been

burned (Joshua 6:24), and that the walls had completely come down (Joshua 6:20).[2] Further examples along these lines can be found in Paul E. Little's book, *Know Why You Believe.*[3]

3) Modern science confirms Bible statements.

Indian sages once taught that the earth was supported by elephants, while the Greeks said that Atlas carried the earth on his back. Yet three thousand years ago, one Bible writer declared: "He suspends the earth over nothing" (Job 26:7). And in the 6th Century A.D. the geographer, Ptolemy, numbered the stars at one thousand. Today, of course, science has confirmed through the aid of powerful telescopes what the prophet said hundreds of years before Christ: "the host of heaven cannot be counted. . . ." (Jeremiah 33:22).

There are passing references in the Word of God about the world being round, (Isaiah 40:22, and Proverbs 8:27)—a piece of knowledge that took science thousands of years to catch up on. In fact, Christopher Columbus was derided and mocked for his belief that the world was a sphere.

For many years the passage of Scripture, "Unless those days be shortened, there should no flesh be saved" (Matthew 24:21-22), seemed absurd. How could there ever come a time when man would be capable of annihilating himself? Even during the Second World War the population of the world increased faster than the ravages of war could decrease it. But then came the invention of the nuclear bomb. People can no longer say that this Scripture has no meaning. One bomb could annihilate New York or Tokyo, or other great cities whose population exceeds ten million. The nuclear bomb has the power to vaporize things in a large area. Today our nuclear stockpiles, if exploded, could wipe everybody off the face of the planet!

4) Modern medicine also confirms biblical statements.

The following are merely two examples which show that medical science has only this century caught up with that which was recorded by Moses in the Bible four thousand years ago.

If you were a pregnant woman in a maternity ward last century, your chances of dying were one in six. This was mainly because of the physicians' practice of not washing their hands between examining dead bodies and performing pelvic examinations among the living. A young doctor, Ignaz Semmelweis, set up a rule that doctors must wash their hands after touching the dead. Three months after this rule came into effect, only one woman had died out of eighty-four. But what Semmelweis instructed in 1847, God had already set forth in Numbers 19, thirty-two centuries before.

Until comparatively recently, doctors used to let the blood out of sick people as a cure. But today, medical science has realized the error of this practice, thus confirming what Moses wrote centuries ago, "The life of the flesh is in the blood" (Lev.17:11). Blood transfusions are now given on many occasions because the blood carries the power of life to heal, not to sicken.

The two illustrations given above are both from *None of These Diseases*, by Dr. McMillen. I certainly recommend the reading of this book for further examples, proving the value of the divine record from a medical viewpoint.[4]

5) The Bible upholds our conscience concerning sin.

This, I believe, is an outstanding reason why it is so easy to believe in the Bible. For what good would holy writings be if they advocated murder, lust, greed, rape and violence? "The law of the Lord is perfect . . . the commandment of the Lord is pure . . . " (Psalm 19:7-8). We know the Bible is the Word of God because its moral teachings have the same law and order as there is in the physical universe—perfect beauty and symmetry. No wonder Scripture is to be desired more than much fine gold! (Psalm 19:10).

6) Fulfilled prophecy.

The overwhelming number of fulfilled Biblical predictions in detail prove that the Bible is the Word of God. It does not take much to be able to predict generalities such as: "One day you will meet a fine young lady and marry her," or to have predicted President Marcos of the Philippines would leave office. It is not sufficient to say that the Bible is inspired because of fulfilled prophecy, and then not be able to give a number of examples. The examples abound. Consider the predictions concerning the coming of Christ that were literally fulfilled.

He was born in Bethlehem (Micah 5:2, fulfilled in Matthew 2:1). He was of the line of David (Isaiah 11: 1-5, fulfilled in Matthew 1:1). He was of the tribe of Judah (Genesis 49:10, fulfilled in Luke 3:33). He was born of a virgin (Isaiah 7:14, fulfilled in Matthew 1:18-23). He ministered in Zebulun in Naphtali which is Galilee (Isaiah 9: 1-2; Matthew 4:12-16).

He was a prophet (Deut. 18:15, fulfilled in Acts 3:19-26). He was rejected by the Jews (Isaiah 53:3, fulfilled in John 1:11). He entered Jerusalem on a young ass (Zech. 9:9, fulfilled in John 12: 13-14). He was sold for thirty pieces of silver (Zech. 11:12, fulfilled in Matthew 26:15). He suffered for our sin (Isaiah 53:4, fulfilled in I Peter 2:24). He rose from the grave (Psalm 16:10, fulfilled in Acts 2:24-32). He ascended into Heaven (Psalm 68:18, fulfilled in Acts 1:9-11).

And we have only mentioned just a few of the fulfilled prophecies concerning Jesus Christ. In his book, *Science Speaks,* Peter Stoner applies the modern science of probability to just eight of these prophecies, and states that the chances of Jesus fulfilling all eight would be one in a hundred quadrillion. (that's 100,000,000,000,000,000).[5] Stoner suggests that if we were to use that many silver dollars, they would cover the entire State of Texas to a depth of two feet! The chances of all eight prophecies being fulfilled in Jesus would be like marking one of those silver dollars, then blindfolding someone and asking that person to walk through the State of Texas to find that marked coin!

7) Jesus Christ referred to the Old Testament with complete confidence that it was the Word of God.

This is yet another wonderful reason why we can have confidence in the Scriptures—this time the Old Testament section of the Bible. Jesus quoted the Old Testament frequently and introduced His teaching at times by the words "It is written . . . ." He encouraged the use of the Scriptures (John 5:39), told the Pharisees they erred because they did not know them (Matt. 22:29), and endorsed them by declaring "The Scripture cannot be broken" (John 10:35).

8) The unity of the Bible is a miracle.

It was written over a period of 1600 years by some 40 different authors in different countries, from different backgrounds and cultures, with little sharing of ideas, and yet it is a complete and perfect whole of truth. Can you imagine 40 authors in different countries writing on the same subject since 400 A.D., and yet they have such a common theme that it dovetails together as a perfect, consistent whole? No wonder the Bible holds a leading place in literature today, and has been translated into well over 1,000 languages.

9) The Bible has been found to be practical in experience.

What the Bible promises concerning our lives is true. Millions have had their lives changed and protected by obeying the Bible's commandments. They have had their prayers answered, their needs provided and their fears relieved. Dr. McMillen declares that over half the diseases and sorrows of the human race would be wiped away if people would just follow the teachings of Jesus. This is quite aside from miraculous intervention in divine healing. It is very practical to believe the Bible.

10) The sick are healed when we lay hands on them and see them recover.

When blind eyes are opened and the deaf receive their hearing, this proves the reliability of the teachings of Jesus Christ and the other Bible writers.

These ten reasons are not the only ones, but they should prove sufficient for the honest inquirer. There are numerous other examples that we can give apart from the ones mentioned here. Take mental and written note of them as you come across them, so that you can use them at a moment's notice as you witness.

---

1. Taken from the NIV Study Bible, p. 5. Copyright 1985 by the Zondervan Corporation. Used by permission.
2. Thompson Chain Bible, (B.B. Kirkbride Bible Co., 1964) p. 338.
3. Paul E. Little, "Know Why You Believe," (Downers Grove, Ill., InterVarsity Press).
4. Dr. S.I. McMillen, "None Of These Diseases," (Old Tappan, New Jersey, Fleming Revell, 1963).
5. Peter Stoner, "Science Speaks," (Chicago, Moody Press).

All royalties of this printing will go to the Shelling Memorial Scholarship Fund at Pacific & Asia Christian University, to assist Filipino students attending certain PACU courses. Should you wish to further contribute to this fund please write or contact:

Shelling Memorial Scholarship Fund
Pacific & Asia Christian University
75-5851 Kuakini Highway
Kailua-Kona, HI 96740-2199
(808) 326-7228

You may purchase these books from the following distributors in your country:

USA
Frontline Communications
P.O. Box 55787
Seattle, Washington 98155
(206) 771-1153

AUSTRALIA
Christian Marketing
P.O. Box 154
North Geelong, VIC 3215
(052) 78-6100

CANADA
Scripture In Song
P.O. Box 550
Virgil, ONT LOS 1TO
(416) 468-4214

ENGLAND
Mannafest Books
Holmsted Manor, Staplefield Rd.
Cuckfield, W. Sussex RH17 5JF
(0444) 440229

GERMANY
Youth With A Mission
Military Ministries
Mozart Str. 15
8901 Augsburg — Stadtbergen
(0821) 522659

HOLLAND
Pelgrim Intl. Boekenckm
Rijnstraat 12
6811 EV Arnheim

HONG KONG
Jensco, Ltd.
G.P.P Box 1987
3-3113768

NEW ZEALAND
Concord Distributors, Ltd.
Private Bag
Havelock North
(070) 778-161

SOUTH AFRICA
Mannafest Media
Private Bag X0018
Delmas 2210
(0157) 3317

OTHER LIFE-CHANGING BOOKS BY YOUTH WITH A MISSION AUTHORS:

____copy (copies) of **ANCHOR IN THE STORM,** Helen Applegate with Renee Taft. The gripping true story of how Helen and her husband, Ben, Captain of the mercy ship, the M/V Anastasis, persevere through insurmountable odds to hold on to their dream to serve God on the high seas. @5.95 = ____

____copy (copies) of **ASIA: A CHRISTIAN PERSPECTIVE,** by Mary Ann Lind, a Ph.d in Asian history. Creative strategies for reaching Asia with the gospel, where over two-thirds of the world live, from the mud-walled villages in Bangladesh to the gleaming skyscrapers in Singapore. Learn what vital role you can play in seeing the Great Commission fulfilled.
@7.85 = ____

____copy (copies) of **BRINGIN' 'EM BACK ALIVE,** by Danny Lehmann, director of Youth With A Mission in Honolulu, Hawaii. Practical, bold, easy to read and use in teaching others how to win hearts to a loving God. @5.95 = ____

____copy (copies) of **COUNSELING THE HOMOSEXUAL**, by Mike Saia, who has an active counseling and teaching ministry, and who has worked with YWAM in Holland, Germany and Sunland, California, where he presently lives. A sensitive, accurate and biblical manual for pastors, counsellors and families. @$8.95 = ____

____copy (copies) of **THE FATHER HEART OF GOD,** by Floyd McClung, Executive Director of YWAM. How to know God as a loving, caring Father and a healer of our hurts.
@$4.95 = ____

____copy (copies) of **FATHER, MAKE US ONE**, by Floyd McClung. Firsthand, personal illustrations on how you can experience the healing power of God's love and unity in the Body of Christ. @$5.95 = ____

____copy (copies) of **FLOWERS FROM THE BRIDGE—Milestones to Overcoming Grief,** by Renee Taft, who works with the Communication and Performing Arts Colleges at

Pacific and Asia Christian University in Hawaii. The true story of how Renee and her family experienced the loss of a loved one and discover 12 milestones to healing.   @$5.95 = _____

_____copy (copies) of **GO MANUAL.** This manual has been produced with the desire to see people of all walks of life involved in missions. It lists over 2,500 short- and long-term opportunities and further training possibilities in over 60 countries, involving more than 140 YWAM locations.
@$1.95 = _____

_____copy (copies) of **INTIMATE FRIENDSHIP WITH GOD,** by Joy Dawson, a dynamic communicator and teacher. Keys to knowing, obeying and loving God.   @$5.95 = _____

_____copy (copies) of **IS THAT REALLY YOU, GOD?,** Loren Cunningham with Janice Rogers. The exciting beginnings of Youth With A Mission as Loren Cunningham discovers keys to hearing God's voice.   @$5.95 = _____

_____copy (copies) of **LIVING ON THE DEVIL'S DOORSTEP,** by Floyd McClung. Join Floyd and his wife, Sally, as they live first in a hippie hotel in Afghanistan and then next door to prostitutes, pimps, drug dealers and homosexuals in Amsterdam.   @$8.95 = _____

_____copy (copies) of **PERSONAL PRAYER DIARY—DAILY PLANNER.** A quiet time journal using a week-at-a-glance format that allows a daily record of your times alone with God. Ideal for home, office or as a gift. Great for busy people!
@$9.95 = _____

_____additional copy (copies) of **WE CANNOT BUT TELL**
@$5.95 = _____

_____copy (copies) of **WINNING, GOD'S WAY,** Loren Cunningham with Janice Rogers. How you can experience a victorious Christian life as you discover new freedom, joy and power through living God's way.   @$5.95 = _____

_____copy (copies) 6-cassette album of **ARE THERE ANSWERS...To the Difficult Questions People Ask?** by Loren Cunningham. 1)Can You Prove There Is a God? 2)What

Loren Cunningham. 1)Can You Prove There Is a God? 2)What Kind of Personality Does God Have? 3)Why the Cross? 4) Creating With God 5) Why War? 6) How Can a God of Love Send a Man To Hell?   @$24.95 = _____

_____copy (copies) 6-cassette abum of **LET'S TURN THE WORLD AROUND,** by Loren Cunningham. 1)Let's Turn the World Around, 2) Let's Go Barefoot, 3)Conditions For Knowing God's Voice, 4)Creating With God, 5) Go Means a Change of Location, 6)Releasing the Power of the Spirit.
@$24.95 = _____

$2.00 postage for 1-2 books/cassette albums plus .25 for each additional book.

<u>Quantity Discounts</u>

10-25 items	**20% discount**
25 items or more	**42% discount**

For Visa/MasterCard orders only call 1-800-922-2143

ORDER NOW!

Send your payment to:

Frontline Communications — YWAM
P.O. Box 55787
Seattle, Washington 98155
(206) 771-1153

_____ Enclosed is $_____
Name

_____
Address

_____
City and State   Zip Code